PICASSO

THE LATER

YEARS

By Chris Wade

PICASSO: THE LATER YEARS

Wisdom Twins Books, 2018

wisdomtwinsbooks.weebly.com

This edition released in 2018

Text Copyright of Chris Wade, 2018

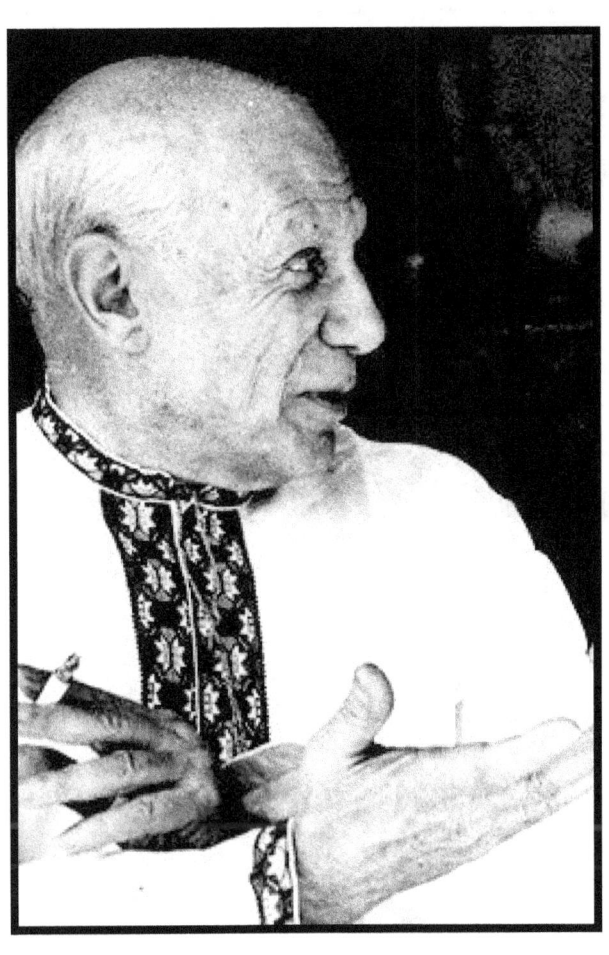

PICASSO

THE LATER YEARS

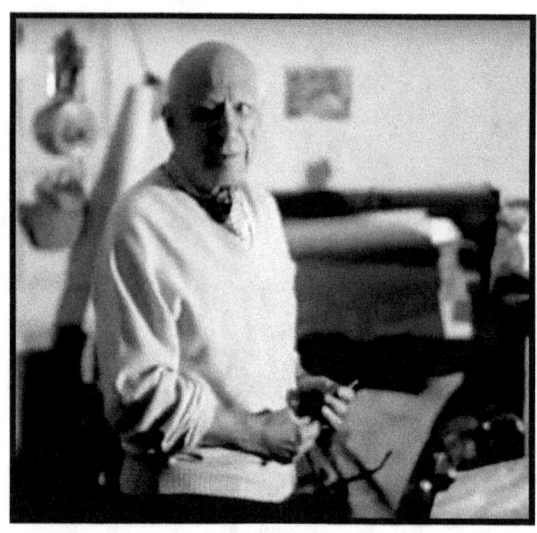

CONTENTS

4

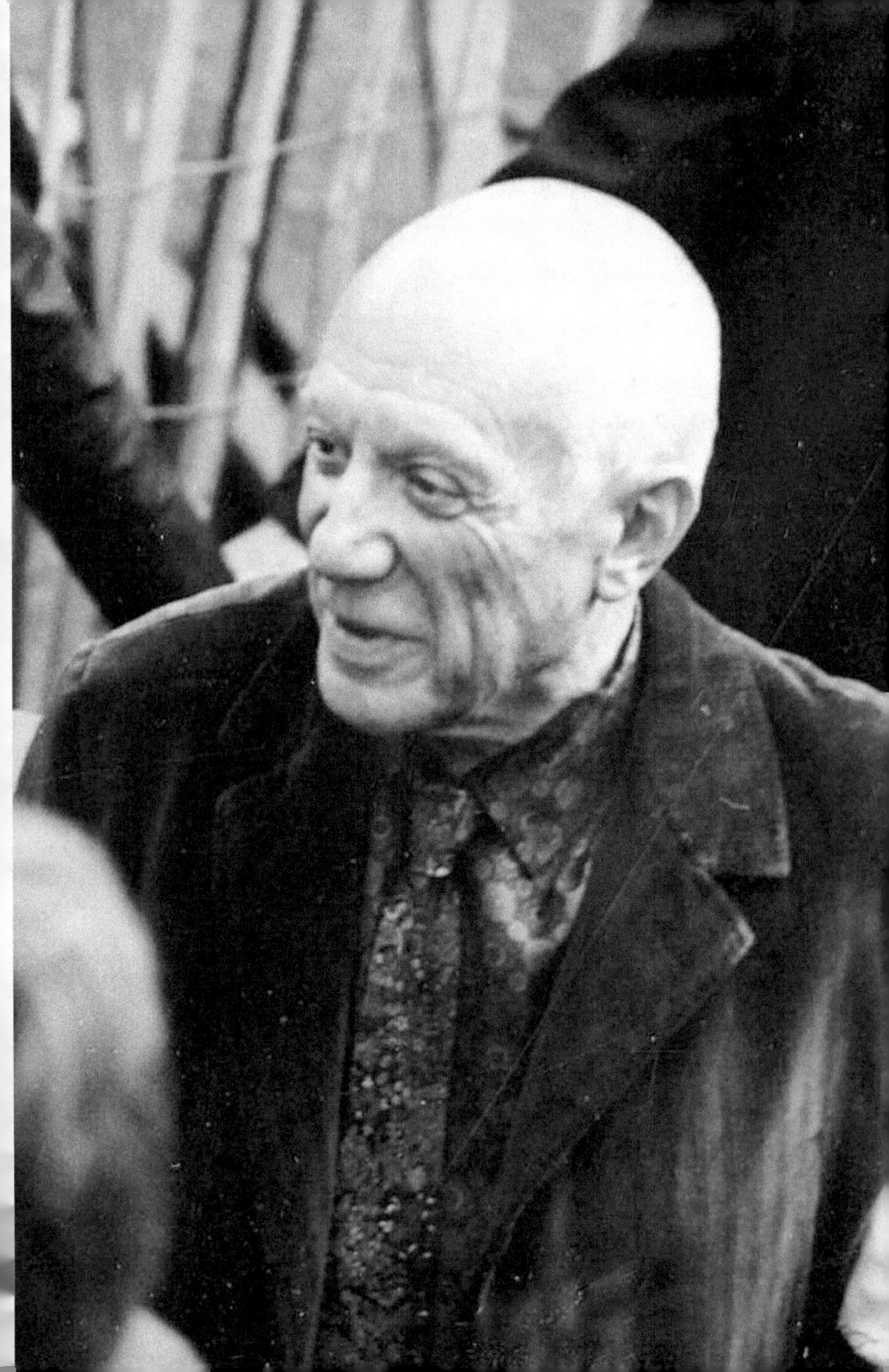

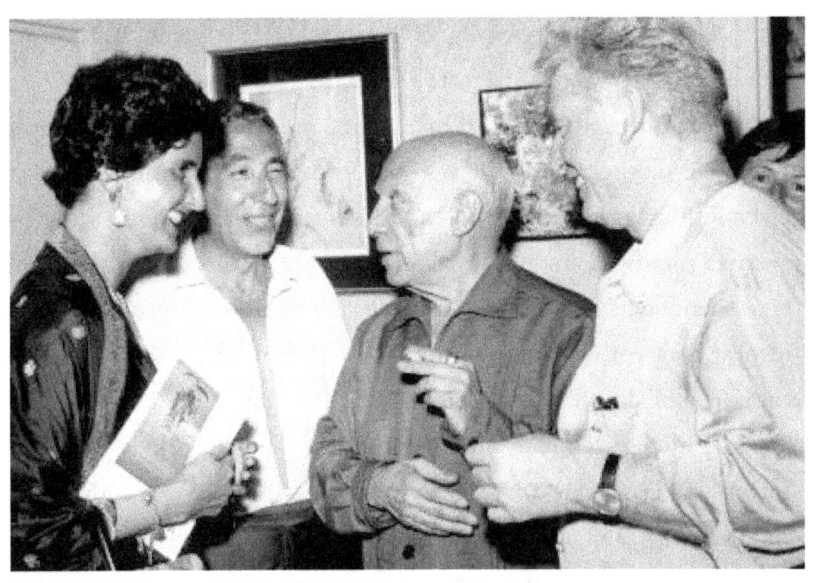

INTRODUCTION

An Artist Facing Death

**"The older you get the stronger the wind gets -
and it's always in your face."**

The life of Pablo Picasso, the iconic and legendary artist who chronicled the 20th century in his paintings and sculptures, was a long, epic, winding and turbulent story. As an artist and man, Picasso went through so many stages, moods and varied directions that admirers can have the luxury of picking a favourite era, a favourite muse, a favourite wife, a favourite collection of paintings, a favourite house, and so on. One can also easily fall into the trap of putting each phase of his life into tidy sections (Blue Period, Cuist Period etc.), when in fact the developments were more organic and subtle. But

7

that's an understandable way to lean, especially when it becomes impossible to separate facts from the irresistible Picasso myth.

That said, just look through his life and you will see one redefining age after another, and in each time span Picasso not only stays relevant, but changes the rules, and importantly makes new ones. He invented totally new styles of painting, whole genres in fact, which he then abandoned for the next discovery, the newest inspiration and freshest perspective on his journey to find - or at last understand - the truth. And he did this, remarkably so, right up until his death.

As the ageing legend - that familiar stocky figure in a striped T shirt, as cool as can be, always staring the camera down with sturdy defiance - Picasso knew he was untouchable. He has been put up on a pedestal, an artist beyond criticism and reach, where every stroke of his brush was lauded as an act of genius, dissected with obsession. "I can say shit to anyone," he famously said. Even when some less than savoury details about his life came to public knowledge (in great part thanks to his ex wife Francoise Gilot, with her 1964 book Life with Picasso), Pablo's credibility as an artist remained intact. Only when he reached very near the end with his final paintings did the critics and doubters dare to question his work. But forty odd years later, even *those* paintings have been embraced, seen as a fitting final footnote to a career which is beyond rivalry in the 20th century. At the time though, Picasso's last works were seen as the inane scribblings of a dirty old man, dripping with morbid sexuality, done in poor taste and a shadow of what had come before. And what had come before? Well, a towering and intimidating past, that's what; and in order to understand Picasso's later stance as an old icon whose best work was arguably behind him (though I disagree), you must look into the past. And Picasso's past is our own past.

He was born in Malaga, Spain, in 1881. Pablo was initially dead for a matter of minutes before calling out his first wail, signalling his reluctant arrival into the world he would help change in the forthcoming century. Baptized a Catholic, Picasso later became a firm atheist, though he remained in other ways a very superstitious man, a God fearing non-believer as it were. His father Don Jose taught art, but his views on painting were from a strictly traditional and academic angle. Behind closed doors however, he was a passionate painter, though he never broke away from teaching and became a fully fledged artist in his own right. He wanted great things for his son, but Pablo would have to follow his father's rules to reach this desired goal. Obsessed with painting pigeons, Picasso's father once left a pair of severed pigeon feet by a canvas and asked his young son to paint them while he was out. According to Picasso, he did them so well that when his father returned he gave Picasso his paints, said he didn't need them anymore and vowed never to paint again. This is Picasso folk lore of course, and a ludicrous myth enhanced by the man himself; but it makes for a fantastic story. What is believed to be true however, is the fact that his first word was 'pencil'. He was a compulsive drawer, driven by his need to create on the page the objects he saw in his life, and by the age of ten had already mastered form and perspective. "I never drew like a child," he famously said, "I drew like Raphael." While not totally true judging by the early works that have survived, Picasso did become a master early on, remarkably so in fact, and he certainly had a gift from the word go. It did not take long before others outside the home realised this fact.

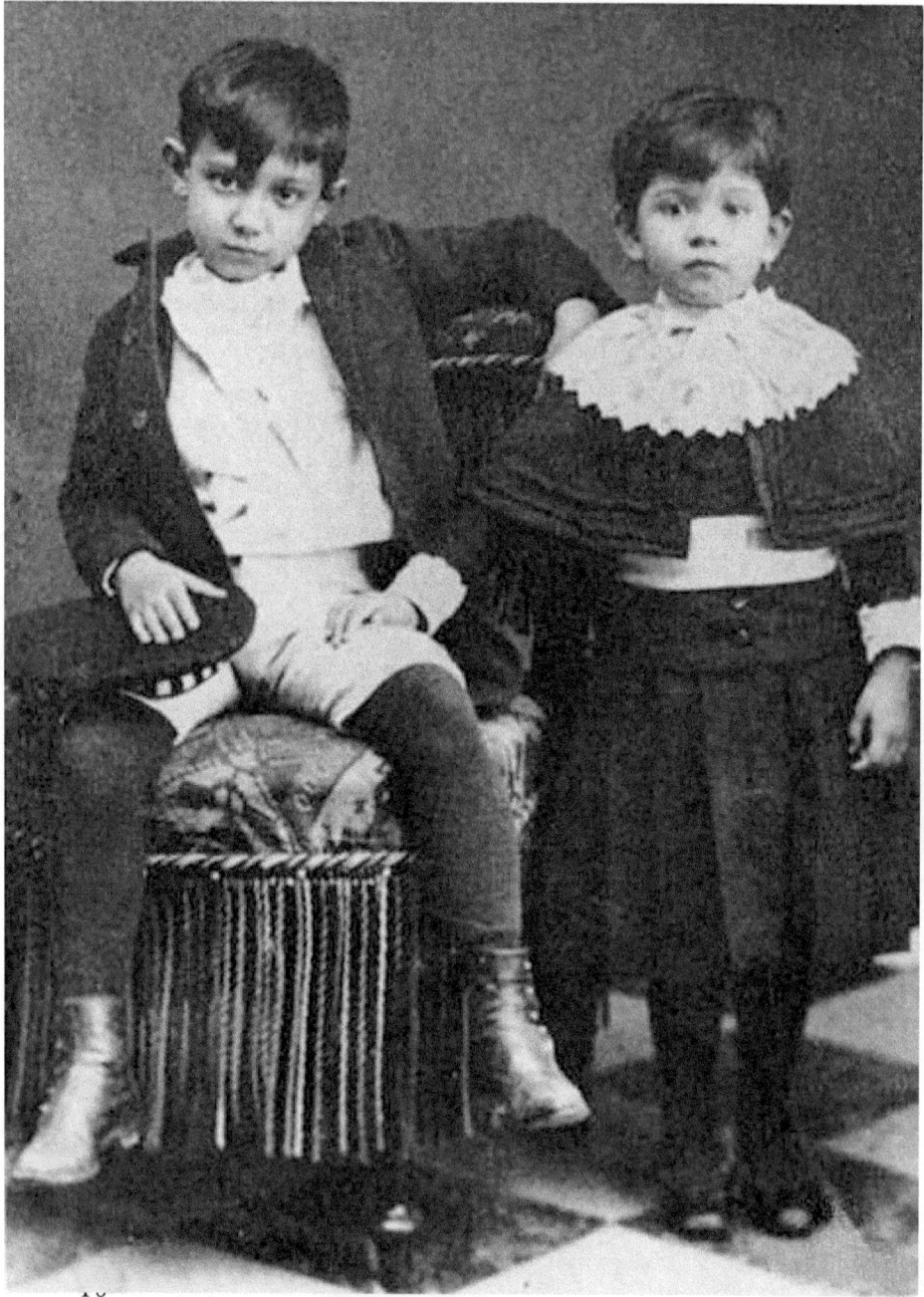

When Pablo was small, the family moved to A Coruna on the coast, where his father became a professor at the School of Fine Arts. With his two sisters Lola and Conchita, Picasso was saddened to leave behind his beloved Malaga, but as his views were so set firmly on art, he did not dwell on his lost birth town for too long. He took classes with his father, mastered drawing, and began to paint with oil, starting with family portraits. But an early tragedy shook his world. His sister Conchita fell ill, and when she was dying, in desperation Pablo asked God to save her. Reaching out to the Lord, he said he would give up art if he spared Conchita's life. The fact that God showed no mercy explains Picasso's sudden compulsive urge to create from here after - and of course his subsequent atheist outlook.

The family did not stay put in A Coruna for too long. Again, Jose took another job, this one at the School of Fine Arts in Barcelona, a city Picasso loved for all its vitality, culture, art and action. When looking back as an older man, even from Paris, he regarded Barcelona as his true spiritual home. "There is where it all began," he later said. "There is where I understood how far I could reach"

But his stay in Barcelona was cut short when Pablo was sent to "study" art in Madrid, starting his course in 1897. He hated his time there, and eventually stopped going to classes, spending most of his time in the El Prado Museum, gazing at the works of Goya, Velazquez and El Greco for hours, inspired by the magic they created on canvas. Later that year, with his friend Manuel Pallares, Picasso escaped Madrid, staying in Pallares' home village of Horta de Ebro. It was a vital eight months, and Picasso later said he learned everything he knew from that village. (He would revisit again a few years later, and paint the town while in his Cubist period.) His work in this era shifted from Realism to something deeper, with Symbolist tendencies. His work in 1897 - or what has survived of it - is not what the world would instantly recognise as Picasso, there being a more dramatic element to the work. Science and Charity, which achieved acclaim at the time and made people take notice of Pablo, depicted a doctor by the bed of a dying woman. For the face of the man of medicine, Pablo turned to his father for inspiration. It remains an intensely powerful painting and a sombre pre cursor, in mood at least, to his Blue Period. Other works, like Man in a Park and 1898's Portrait of Lola, are subtle and tasteful, but Picasso was still learning how to get what he felt on paper and make it a reality.

Pablo then headed out to Paris to find himself, and to experience as many adventures as he could. Sparking up a friendship with the poet Max Jacob, who educated Picasso in the Parisian ways, he began to spread his wings, both personally and artistically. They soon got a place together, and Picasso would stay up painting all through the night. He was extremely poor in this period, but looked back upon the early Parisian days fondly, because it was here that he realised art could be both important and personal; and the more personal the art got, the more it grew in importance. He also discovered the fairer sex and would frequent whore houses to quench his desires.

In the second year of the 20th century, Picasso, then in his early twenties, went through his much celebrated Blue Period, a three year age of gloom brought about by the suicide of a friend, Carlos Casagemas, an undeniably inspiring and vital point in his life. Carlos was having certain personal problems, and he could not woo the object of his desire, Germaine Pichot, who he thought was mocking him for his inability to be a man in the truest sense. Enraged one day, he marched into a tavern, armed, and aimed his pistol at her head. It narrowly missed her, so quickly he turned the gun on himself and pulled the trigger. Picasso was out of Paris at the time, and was tortured, for he knew that if he had been by his friend's side, such a thing would not have happened. Still, Picasso's reaction to this vile tragedy was to move into his friend's apartment, as the rent was paid up for a few months, and shack up with Germaine himself. Perhaps Picasso's torn emotions at the time are what led him into the very un-commercial Blue Period, and maybe he had a sense of guilt for not only living in his dead friend's home, but also making love to the woman his fallen comrade could never win for himself. Though there is no sudden overnight entry into this stage of painting, and indeed it is a gradual development over the space of months, Picasso's work does become cold, terrifying and hopelessly dark in the aftermath, though still beautiful at the same time. Some of the strongest paintings in Picasso's life were created in the bleakness following the incident, such as his Blue Period Self Portrait (1901), 1903's The Old Guitarist and the stunning La Vie (1903), which depicts the impotent Casagemas with the girl he tried to kill, facing the image of a new born baby, tormented and ridiculed by his flaccidity. The incident scarred Picasso and kept him blue for three years. Still, the tragedy resulted in his first series of serious works.

When the clouds of doom lifted, he went through his brighter Rose Period, a time of greater understanding, up until 1906. Though again there is not a click of a finger to set Picasso into his new brighter phase, there is a certain light coming back into the work in 1904. Picasso focused on blindness, acrobats and harlequins in his new works, and though the colours were more vibrant and warm, there was still a heavy feeling of sadness, this time in the fact that like Picasso, these travelling performers and actors were also away from home, perhaps a little lost, despite what they presented to the world on the exterior. It's a colourful, moody, atmospheric era of Picasso's painting timeline, and it was while creating these works that he began to build up a proper reputation in Paris. People started collecting his work, and around this time he met fellow artist Henri Matisse at a Gertrude Stein gathering, with whom he maintained a life long rivalry and playful friendship. As it happens, Stein was a vital figure in this era too, becoming Pablo's main patron and supporter, introducing him to more influential people in the art world.

In 1907 he began to be inspired by primitive art, and delivered some of the most memorable paintings of all time under its influence, such as Les Demoiselles d'Avignon. This "African" era begins with the iconic work, depicting nude prostitutes in a brothel, their faces distorted and harshly uninviting, stories told in their twisted features. Unlike earlier art depicting female nudity, Picasso's whores were confrontational, raw, ugly even, and their penetrating eyes stared out at you with harsh judgement. Importantly, it was in the style of the painting that Picasso found a new approach, rather than merely the subject matter and tonal mood. He had been visiting an African art museum at Palais du Trocadero when he had what he called a revelation. Immediately, his work began to mirror the primitive look and feel of the Africans. The piece had come about when Picasso vowed to create a work that would rival, if not beat Matisse in the avant-garde stakes, and see him over take Henri as the leading artist of the time. When the painting was unveiled, it caused

14

an outrage, and Picasso's aims came to fruition. He was now the most exciting painter around, pushing the envelope with every new turn.

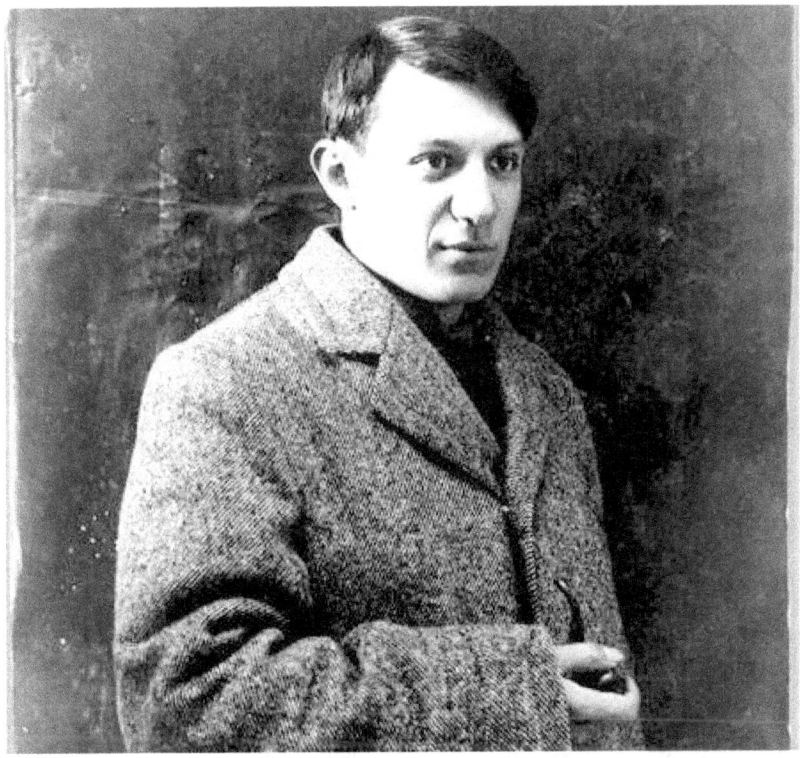

Picasso in 1908.

He wasn't going to stop at African primitivism for too long though, for the ever keen Picasso was out for new discoveries. With his artist friend Georges Braque, he dove head on into Cubism, firstly as an analytical study, then as a full on exploration in the years leading up to the 1920s. This was an attempt to deconstruct the laws of paint, the logic of traditional structure and to shake up the art establishment. This work was met with great shock at the time, but within a few years Cubism became an accepted style in its own right. "People need to be woken up," he later said. "Their way of identifying things, shattered. Unacceptable images should be created."

It seems that at every turn, Picasso was turning the whole art world on its head. That's not to say he did not respect the old guard, because he certainly did, and celebrated tradition in his neoclassical period in the 1920s, while also being welcomed into the circle of the Surrealists by Andre Breton, who saw his revolutionary style as a part of the movement's outlook. By now Picasso was world famous and making serious money from his art, though he did not submit to popularity and begin to repeat himself. He strode on into a new decade after a successful ten years as the world's premier painter, bringing classical disciplines to modern times. The restless creator had new horizons to explore.

In the 1930s, Picasso made some of his strongest and most famous work, such as the powerful Guernica (1937), dedicated to the devastated village in Spain which suffered greatly during the Civil War. Picasso famously holed himself up in Paris while the Germans occupied his beloved city, not exhibiting while the Nazis were in power because his work was considered degenerate. It was an enthralling time for Pablo. Food was scarce but he soldiered on, painting on ply wood when canvases were not available to him. While carrying on with his life as best he could, Picasso was experiencing harassment, but remaining head strong, garnering huge respect for staying put and not abandoning his adopted homeland in its hour of need. When his apartment was searched by the Germans one day, a solider held up a copy of Guernica and asked Picasso if he had done it. "No," Picasso replied with defiance, "you did!"

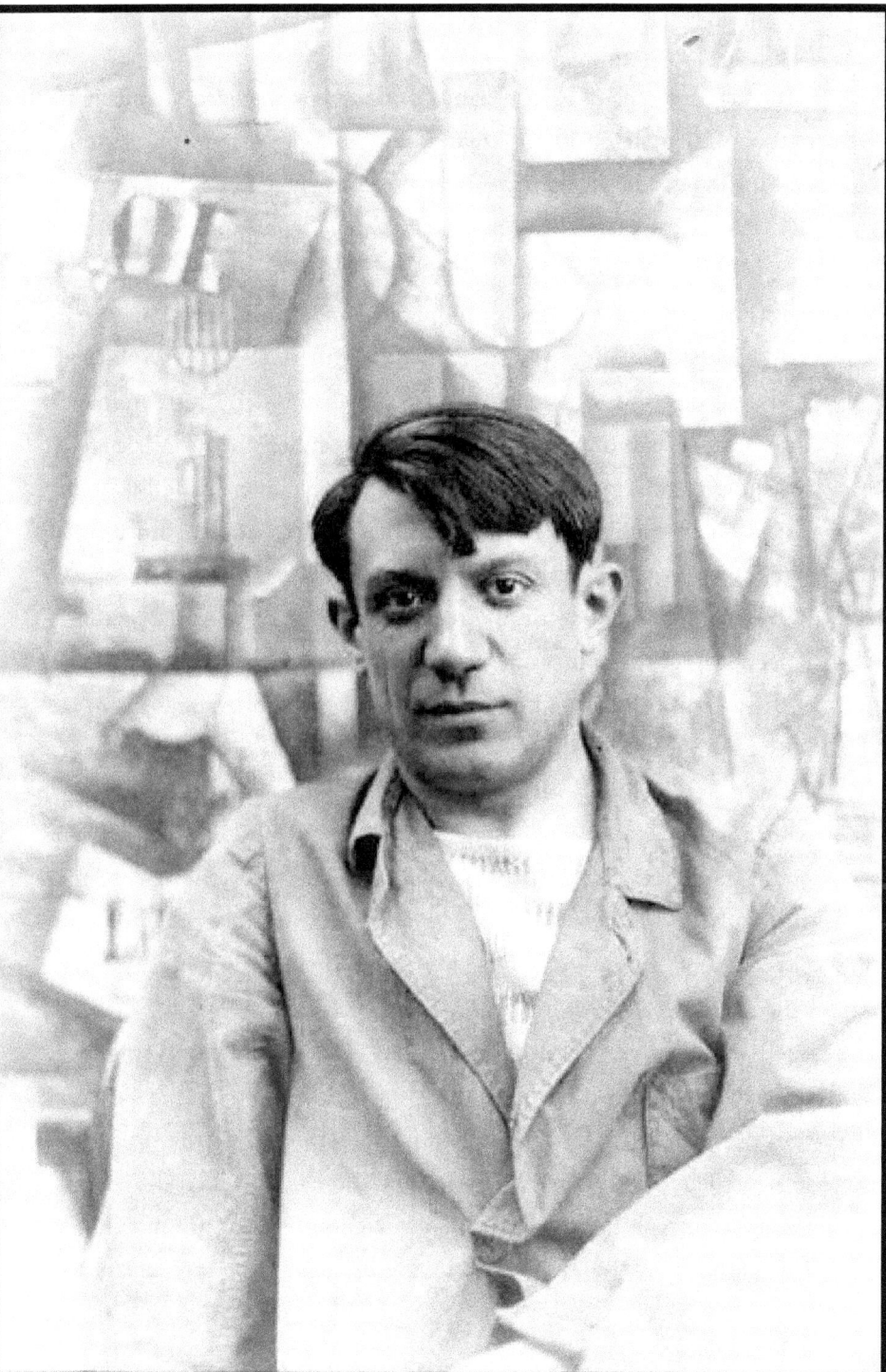

During this era, Picasso became something of a hero, a renegade outlaw who went on living, loving and painting despite the turmoil and upset outside the confines of his studio. Then again, his personal life was hardly peaceful either. He was still legally wed to his first wife, Olga Khokhlova, but living with Marie-Therese Walter, who bore him a child, and seeing the photographer and poet Dora Maar on the side, the woman who remained his true muse through the war years. It was she who documented the creation of his landmark Guernica, a painting which became a symbol for peace, and a reminder of the horrors man carelessly inflicts upon his fellow man. Asked about each isolated image in the picture, and to sum up the symbolism as best he could, Picasso remained enigmatic. "It isn't up to the painter to define the symbols," he offered. "Otherwise it would be better if he wrote them out in so many words! The public who look at the picture must interpret the symbols as they understand them."

By now, Picasso was the world's most loved and famous artist, and his admirers waited with bated breath for what he would come up with next. During the liberation of Paris in 1944, Picasso was freed once again, and able to live life as he once had. By the end of the 1940s, though approaching old age, Picasso was as vital, free and passionate as ever before, enjoying life as an internationally adored artist, painting and having affairs like a man half his age. By the mid 1940s, Picasso had outgrown his mistress Dora Maar, and was in a deep relationship with aspiring art student Francoise Gilot, who bore him two children, Claude and Paloma. Picasso enjoyed the liberating joys of being with the much younger Francoise, and relished his second chance at fatherhood. The fact she was a strong woman in her own right though, and failed to be the unquestioning worshipper he needed a wife to be, made sure that life was not always going to run smoothly for the pair. They split in 1954. "Women are machines for suffering," he told her.

By then, Picasso had reached the grand old age of seventy; but of course, in typical fashion, he did not slow down. If anything, he upped his work rate, and though a concerned and empathetic man to the plight of the outside world, his artistic environment became inspired more than ever by his enclosed personal surroundings. This millionaire Communist lived in a bubble of creativity, sculpting, painting and entertaining all day and night. It was a life he had chosen and was destined to live out.

As he grew older still, Picasso cut the world out even more. With his second wife Jacqueline Roque, whom he married in 1961 (decades his junior - she was in her mid thirties, he was eighty), Picasso began a new chapter which lasted until his last day on earth. The loved up doting wife cared for him like a child, always looking out for his best interests and ensuring the increasingly elderly Picasso's life was in order. Though she shut out his family and sparked much controversy within Picasso's circle, she certainly cared for her husband. It was all about making sure he was still able to be creative, that no one would disturb him from his work... and work he certainly did.

This brings me to the point I was making at the start of this introduction. Picasso had gone through so many women, so many artistic phases and so many adventures, that it seems odd that the period I am most fascinated with is the latter one, which saw Picasso creating more personal, confessional, fearful, often frightening work, and keep up this vitality until his death in 1973, at the age of 91. It is, essentially, the Jacqueline era, an era which is sadly too often overlooked.

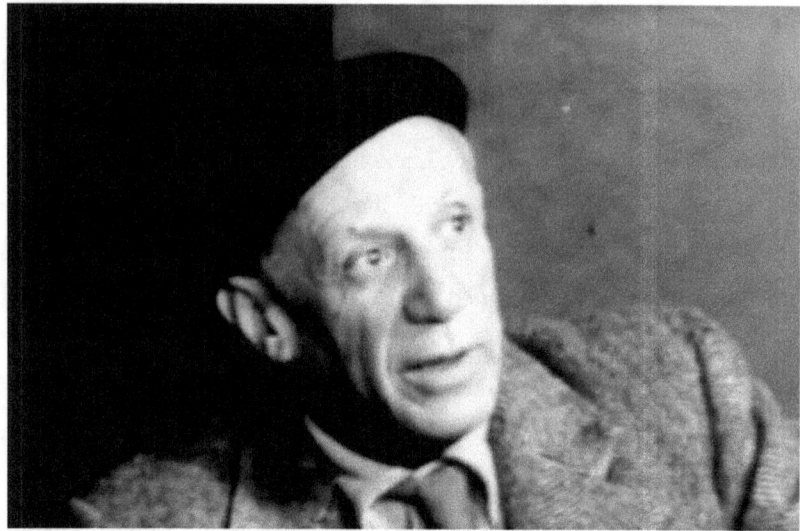

But it remains a remarkable time frame, and an inspiring one too. Footage of the elderly Picasso at work or relaxing at home presents a man not dimmed by the passing of time. Indeed, he still looks like that young artist who changed the rules and pushed the boundaries. In those crackly home movies, the old Picasso seems so alive and present with the observer that it's actually rather haunting observing him in his daily activities, with those huge black eyes staring into the camera as if to challenge the viewer. "Look at me," he seems to say, threatening us to face up to the inevitability of time, age, experience, and the impending doom of death - always around the corner, just out of sight but almost within reach.

Picasso's last decades are exciting, atmospheric, controversial, eventful and fascinating to delve into. Unlike that other great 20th Century Spanish artist, Salvador Dali, who wasted away in his own self-made museum as an old man, Picasso refused to acknowledge the world that honoured him, staying in the tortured comforts of his studio, indulging his endless curiosity, making a diary of his life in art; working, working, working.

In a series of articles and essays, this book explores that special era and celebrates the closing chapters of an iconic life. Given that his last phase is gaining more appreciation as the years go on, it seems an appropriate time to take a closer look at the final act of Picasso's story, just before the curtain came down forever.

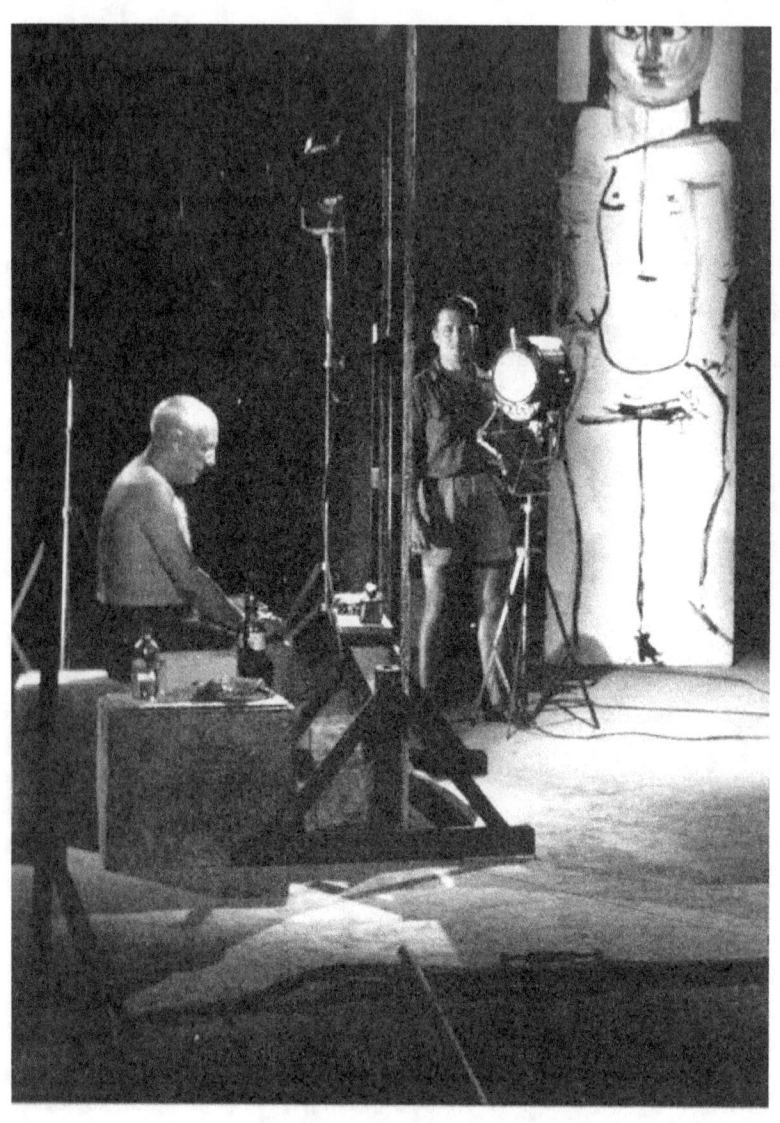

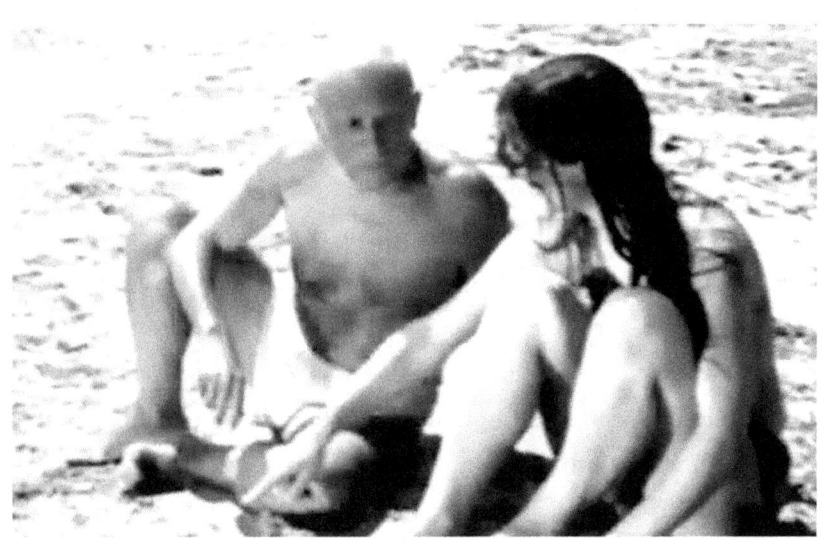

"NO ONE LEAVES A MAN LIKE ME"

Francoise Gilot and Pablo Picasso

"I knew it was going to be a catastrophe, but a catastrophe worth living." - Francoise Gilot

The pairing of Pablo Picasso and Francoise Gilot represents what is possibly the most iconic merging of love, intellectual understanding and mutual creativity in art history. Their initial meeting was romantic and organic, though still macho in the truest sense; in typical style of the Malagan male, Picasso had seen her from afar and wanted to make her his. They enjoyed a fruitful romance, but their pairing turned sour when Gilot proved too independent in thought and mentality for his tastes, and failed to be the submissive wife Picasso wanted - and needed - in order to remain the unquestionable and unquestioned genius. Surrounded by yes man, Gilot's biggest crime was having the audacity to say no to Pablo every now and then. "There was no winning with him," she later said, "only different ways of losing. And *he* never won either."

The breakdown of Francoise and Pablo's relationship came at a time when Picasso was beginning his seventies, ever more aware of his own mortality. At a time when most men are retreating to the comforts of the arm chair, Picasso was as fiery, unpredictable and creative as ever. The end of their union was painful for Picasso, but it was harder for Francoise, who plucked up the courage and left for the hills with their children in tow. This split splintered his life at a vital time, when Picasso was coming to terms with being an old man, trying to hang on to his youth and the creative gift he had been blessed with. Some say Francoise was the only woman who "survived" Picasso, the one who lived to tell the tale; and assessing the facts judges this argument as well informed.

It's important, when understanding why this split was so important and crushing to Pablo, to rewind ten years earlier when it all began. Francoise Gilot was an aspiring young artist when she first met Picasso in 1943, still only in her early twenties. Now, Francoise is 96, still sharp eyed and alert, though slightly irritated when interviewers only want to ask her about her ten year relationship with Picasso, and not the wonderful art she went on to create herself over the next few decades after Pablo was out of her life, carving a respectable career in her own right. In 1964, a decade after their split, she wrote a memoir of their time together, which for a short time, threatened to darken the artist's reputation as a hero and a man. But as his genius in the art world still remained undimmed, people were willing to over look his

24

darker aspects as a human being, and his credibility remained carved in stone. He was, in short, beyond reproach.

Francoise was studying law in the early 1940s when she passed her exams but failed her orals. In Paris, against the wishes of her father, she became interested in art and making a career in it. As she was firmly in the centre of Parisian art circles by 1943, it was only a matter of time before she would meet Picasso himself. She had an interest in his work, as did any serious painter, though she might have purposely gone the other way in her own style than be directly inspired by him. When Picasso first set his eyes on her in the Paris cafe, she was with her friend Genevieve. He approached her table with a bowl of cherries and plenty of smooth talk, telling Francoise she did not look like a painter. "That is the funniest thing I've ever heard," Picasso was quoted as saying when he heard she was an artist. "Girls who look like you could never be painters." Francoise was at the start of her artistic career, and Picasso had already been painting seriously for almost half a century. As she later said, many of his best works were behind him, while her future was ready and waiting ahead of her. She was confident and had faith in her own abilities. If she had not been, there was no way Francoise would have dared to enter a relationship with Pablo Picasso of all people, the world's most worshipped artist. His casually sexist comment that day in the cafe can be forgiven, for female painters really did *not* look like Françoise at the time. She was, essentially, a forerunner of female art, and one of the first women to be taken seriously in a competitive, formerly male dominated field. Even Picasso had to stand up and pay attention, though he made it clear through their union that she could only have so much acclaim for her work, and it must never compete with his own.

She and her friend visited Pablo the next day after the exchange of cherries and small talk, and it was clear, especially to Picasso, that they were there primarily to see his pictures. Aware of this, and perhaps slightly put out by it, he waited until the last moment before they were about to leave and showed them some work, though only a small number. He told them to return again some time, not as pilgrims just out to see his paintings, but as guests, friends even. If they wanted to see his paintings, they may as well just go to a gallery after all. Taking in Pablo's sincerity, they did return, with Francoise wearing a red dress and delivering red flowers to the master. He laughed, took the flowers and said "women do not bring flowers to an old man like me", but clearly admired her effort, and the fact she had gone to the trouble of matching her outfit to the bouquet.

Pretty soon, Francoise became a part of his inner circle, and she got to know the various characters he had around him. When he first went to kiss her one night, she kissed back without hesitation. Picasso was apparently enraged and appalled that she was so open to his advances, and objected to the fact he did not have to "win" her as it were, to try his luck over a few days and eventually gain her trust as he had with other lovers. The fact Francoise was so sure of herself must have irritated Picasso. After all, she was a modern woman, if not ahead of her time, and Pablo, though still vibrant as a man, was from another age and rather old fashioned.

One night he tried to shock her by reading Marquis de Sade, and when she defiantly said that no one should need to act out such perversity in the bedroom, Picasso's aims became transparent. He too

26

would never dare to attempt any of the sadomasochistic acts in these writings, but thought, as an aging man, that talking about it was shocking enough. The fact he could not outrage the young artist filled him with unrest. Clearly, he had never met a woman like her before, and Picasso told her as much. He said, quite casually, that she was the only woman he had known with her own window to the absolute. Naturally, he was smitten.

Their relationship began naturally as a friendship and developed organically into something much deeper. By 1946, with the Second World War over, she had moved in with him. The beautiful Dora Maar, who had remained Picasso's muse and mistress even through his relationship with Marie-Therese Walker, was now being pushed aside, certainly hurt by the rejection. It was a familiar pattern. After all, Marie-Therese had been 17 when Picasso first met her in 1927, while still married to Olga Khokhlova, and she had been similarly hurt and raging with jealousy when Picasso struck up his intellectual affair with Dora in the mid to late 30s. The repeated cycle began again.

Picasso ensured each woman knew where they stood with him and his life. He had always insisted he never truly loved Dora, but admired her, rather like a friend, someone who he could converse with, who understood art and its importance. Marie-Therese had been the loyal wife, but intellectually she could not hope to match Picasso. Once he realised there was very little there mentally, he went looking, searching if you like, for the match he so pined for. He found it in Dora Maar, but by the mid 1940s he had even grown tired of her, and cast her aside cruelly. To many, she is the ultimate Picasso muse. After all, she was there documenting his work on Guernica, a member of his inner circle as well as a lover and friend. In 1943 though, by which time Dora was in her mid thirties, his attentions turned to Francoise, barely out of her teens, fresh fruit for the picking in his eyes, just like the cherries he brought to her table.

Francoise was different though. She was an artist, a thinker, a deep person of perceptions and understanding, who could be lover, friend, intellectual sparring partner and much more. Perhaps, that given her free spirit and independent mind, she was always destined to be too much for him and his macho, almost brutish attitude towards women and where they belonged. He admired the multi faceted aspects of her personality, but was no doubt challenged by her, disturbed even, by her independence. Still, he was hooked.

Francoise later said that had it not been for the war, she and Picasso's relationship might not have blossomed from an intellectual friendship into a fully blown romance. "Because I would have thought he's very old, I'm very young," she later said. "The men who could've been interested in me, and me in them, just disappeared. It was not a time like any other. It was a time when everything was lost; a time of death. So: do I want to do something before I die, or not? You have to seize it. It was – let's do something right away!"

Francoise began to visit his chateau in North West Paris. "I began to have the feeling that if I looked into a closet, I would find half a dozen ex-wives hanging by their necks," she wrote. "He had a kind of Bluebeard complex that made him want to cut off the heads of all the women he had collected in his little private museum."

Gilot did not inform her parents of her involvement with Picasso, not at first, but when they eventually moved to the South of France, settled down and had two children, Claude and Paloma, they had to be in on her new life. Theirs was not a strictly "passionate" relationship (after all, he was forty years her senior), but together they shared a bond which ran deeper than sex. She was a woman to respect, not one to be dominated, wound up or controlled by her own insecurities. Still, it wasn't through want of trying.

In Francoise, he met his true match. Whereas before he had been able to control and manipulate women into behaving how he wanted them to, opening up their heads and toying with their brains, he was not able to do so with the head strong Francoise. "He did not know me well at all," she once said. "I am very secretive. I smile and I'm polite, but that doesn't mean that I am in agreement, or that I will do as I said I would do. It's just a screen. He thought I would react like all his other women. That was a completely wrong opinion. I had other ideas. I did not put my narcissism in being represented by him. I couldn't care less."

Picasso painted her as he did all the other women who had inspired him, yet she sat for him, as she recalled, only once. He did not use her name in the work, but simply titled it "Portrait de Femme." To him, she was "woman", a female in the truest sense, an amalgamation of everything good, perplexing and enigmatic about femininity.

"But, you know, it was not what we call in French *l'amour fou!* she told the Guardian. "It was an intellectual dialogue as well. I could not say that it was a sentimental love. It was maybe an intellectual love, or a physical love, but certainly not a sentimental love. It was love because we had good reason, each of us, to admire the other."

As the years went on though, Picasso became a tyrant, and by the turn of the 1950s, Francoise was finding life there increasingly tasking. He became abusive and possessive, living up to his self

29

coined nick name the Minotaur. He grew more aggressive as Francoise became less inclined to roll over and take his orders. Though Picasso was a bull like figure with huge influence and power, she did not feel trapped. Picasso was still legally wed to Olga (he refused to divorce her), which certainly made it easier for Francoise to escape life with him. "I was not a prisoner," she said, adding that all she wanted out of Picasso was more affection, being dissatisfied with his treatment of her. "I'd been there of my own will and I left of my own will," she said defiantly. "That's what I told him once, before I left. I said watch out, because I came when I wanted to, but I will leave when I want. He said, Nobody leaves a man like me. I said, we'll see."

She famously exposed Picasso's moodiness, the fact that he would get up as late as possible because he was miserable in the mornings. Up at noon, Picasso would moan and moan, before picking up in the evening. "He was an extremely changeable man." She described his habits in vivid detail, and his more menacing acts; like when he threatened to burn her cheek with a lit cigarette. "But the sadism that he had which was purely mental was even worse later on", Francoise told the Telegraph. "That's why my love for him became extinct. Picasso is certainly the person for whom I had the most intense passion in my whole life, but I was not about to live like a slave in front of a power that had no limit."

She says he wanted her pregnant all the time so she would be weaker, more vulnerable, and he hated it if she dared to say one work was not as good as another. When he did a sculpture of her as a pregnant woman, Francoise admitted she did not care for it. His reaction? To saw its feet off. "I told him, 'I'm here because I love you. But if one day I no longer love you, no power in the world will keep

30

me here, because I am not a sculpture, I can walk with my own two feet.'"

Things began to become unbearable when she learned of his affair with Genevieve Laporte, with whom he took a break in Saint Tropez during 1950s, along with his friend Paul Eluard, while Francoise stayed at home with the kids. Picasso had met her when she interviewed him at 17 for her school paper. He was instantly attracted to her, despite being old enough to be her grandfather. When Picasso returned from his break, Francoise confronted him with the rumours of his affair. He denied it, of course, and even suggested that if he *was* seeing someone else it would also be Francoise's fault too, as much as his own in fact. But worst of all, he made her out to be paranoid and rather silly for believing the gossip. Despite this, she knew the truth, and of course all about his past with women. After all, Picasso was no monk.

With her suspicions in mind, the pair started to drift apart. In time, she even began to hate him, and the thought of getting into bed with Picasso revolted her. Jealousy, by then, was not an emotion she was feeling on any level. Still, he *wanted* her to be jealous, and tried in vein to get at her time and time again. By then though, Francoise had made up her mind.

While Francoise was in Paris doing some designs for a stage show in 1953, Picasso stayed with the children. She was spreading her wings, establishing her life outside his influence. He came out to see her work, bringing the kids with him, knowing that the sight of them might pull at her heart strings. Picasso also gave her a masterfully planned out apology, admitting all he had done wrong in response to a letter she had sent him about the corruption and decay of the love they once had. He confessed about the women, and said he would change. But Francoise could see right through it all, and wasn't ready to buy any of his nonsense. While attention and adoration was poured on her during the opening night of Heracles by her collaborators and well wishers, Picasso was sulking. Clearly, he was not used to playing second fiddle, and while observing the woman who was slipping away from him being embraced by admirers, Picasso was heard to mutter, "Ballets always bring me bad luck." The wheel had turned, and the power balance had shifted.

Given his track record with the fairer sex, Picasso thought he would be able to effortlessly woo her back. But by then Francoise had already met the man she was to leave Picasso for, Kostas Axelos. After she briefly returned to Vallauris for a while to be with the children, Kostas sent her telegrams declaring his love for her. At first they stayed friends, but they soon became lovers. In short, she was playing Picasso at his own game, though not on purpose or out of spite. She was genuinely moved that Kostas had developed feelings for her, and in time she learned to reciprocate them.

The split with Picasso was bitter. Francoise left and took the two children with her, heading back to Paris while Picasso stayed at their home in Vallauris. Even when she had made the train reservations and got the children lined up for Parisian schooling, he did not take her seriously, thinking she would change her mind at the last minute and return to life with him. He was wrong.

Francoise says that she hoped they could remain friends, but it proved difficult, if not impossible. For Picasso, he preferred it if there was no life after him, and he could not bare the idea of her being with anyone else. He would, he said at the time, rather see a woman dead than shacking up with a new man. Picasso was seething and after a couple of months in 1953 complaining to everyone around him - his friends, the court he kept and anyone within ear shot - he began to work his demons out. Alive with rage, jealousy and the feeling he was the one who had been betrayed, he drew like a demon. He was 72 now and clearly from the near two hundred works he did in this short time span, was as inspired as ever, even if the thing that re lit the spark was heart ache and a sense of betrayal. This work was dark, reflecting how Francoise now felt about him. He appears as a joke in these bleakly confessional works, a clownish old man, flabby, unattractive, slightly ludicrous, just as his estranged muse now saw him. As she writhed around with her new lover, Picasso felt a knife in his back; and perhaps for the first time, he felt painfully old. Francoise had left when he was drifting deeper into old age, and as the reaper drew nearer, he was aware that he might have lost some of that old manipulative magic. Rather than thinking Francoise was just stronger than some of the others, Picasso reflected this rejection on himself, essentially seeing himself as the heartbroken victim.

Francoise's affair with Kostas petered out, and Picasso was smug when hearing of the fact. Francoise brought the children to see him and he could not help but rub it in, apparently saying "I knew you wouldn't be able to make out with anyone but me." He went into a long speech, trying to win her round with his wisdom, but when the moment came that Francoise and the children were leaving, he said something which pulled at her heart strings. "We may have had our troubles living together, but it seems to me it's going to be even harder living apart." Still, despite his carefully chosen words, it did not change her mind one bit.

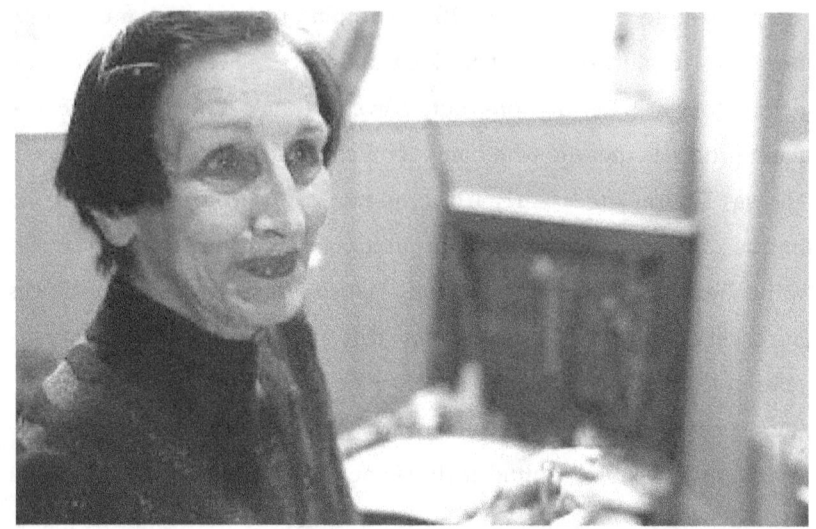

Francoise in 2016.

The break up resulted in the tell-all memoir which both disturbed and crushed Picasso's pride. After all, he wanted his personal home life to remain private, while his art and exaggerated public persona as the bohemian genius did the PR. But Francoise, in his eyes, had crossed the line, even though all she had done was paint a true picture of life with him; in fact, much truer than any work of art could ever be. The book sold boat loads upon its publication, but the former lovers never spoke again.

In the aftermath, as Francoise continued in her painting career, Picasso bad mouthed her to the whole of the art world, trying to sabotage her advancements. But she did not care, moving to America to get away from his influence and remarrying, in 1970, to Jonas Salk. As I write, Francoise still paints every day, and is very much in control of her own legacy and future, even reclaiming many of her old art works at auctions. She will speak of Picasso if she fancies it, or if the interviewer engages her correctly, but for the most part she wants to talk about her own art, her own life, her own experiences, beside the decade she spent with the most famous artist the world has ever known.

For Picasso though, even in the wake of his romance with Francoise, things were about to pick up. While Francoise had been off in Paris for Heracles, Pablo had gotten to know a young girl called Jacqueline Roque. She was only in her mid twenties at the time but during their chats at Madoura Pottery where she worked in 1953, Picasso had been hopelessly charmed by her. As 1953 turned to 54, and Francoise was definitely out of the picture, Picasso knew it was the beginning of a new age, his final chapter, with the loyal young Jacqueline about to take her place as Queen Picasso.

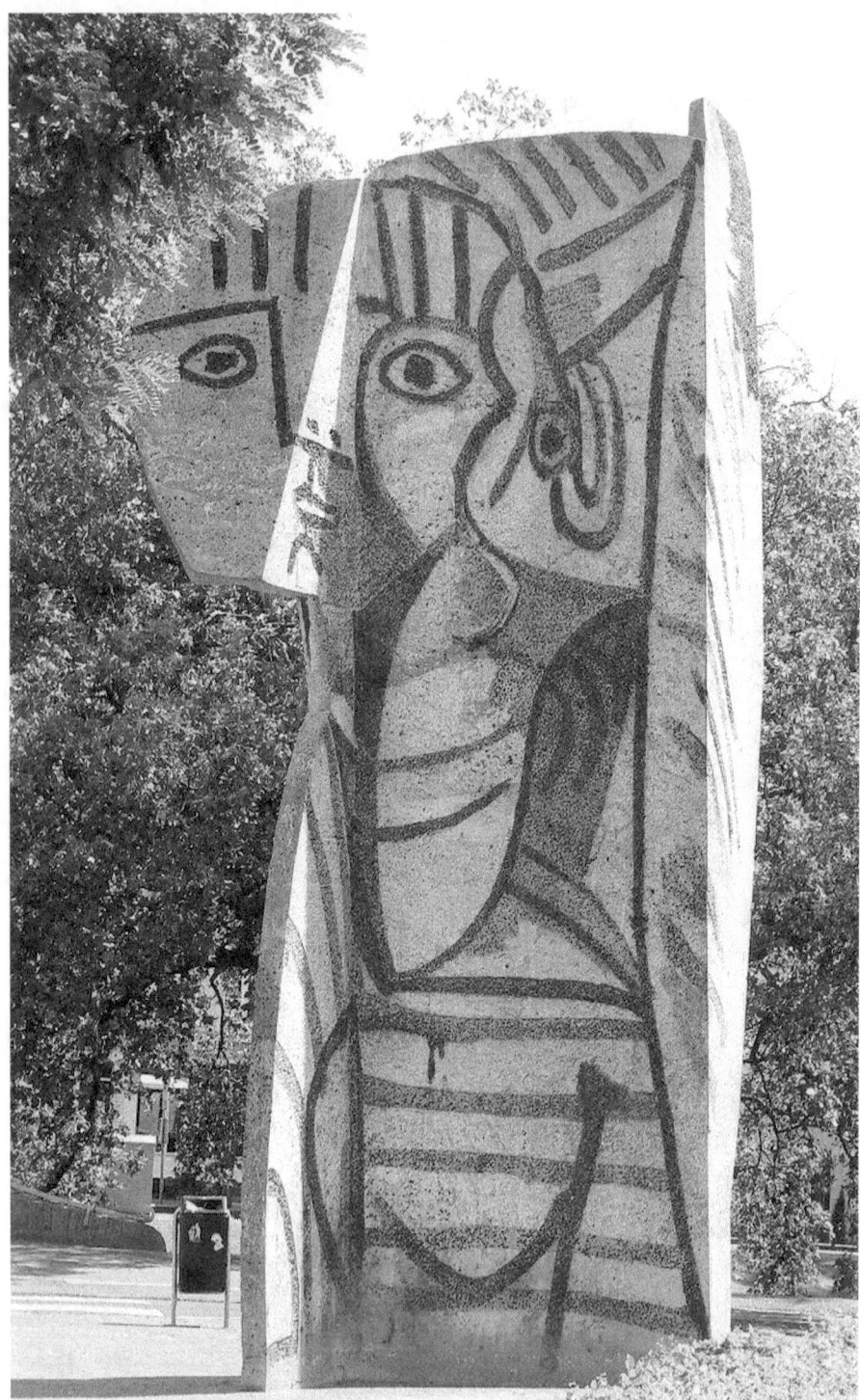

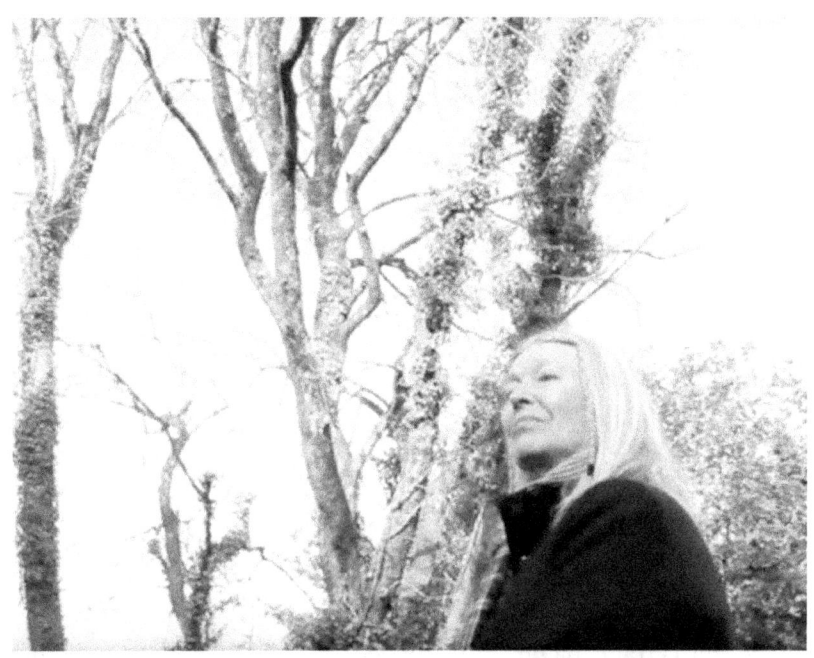

THE BALLAD OF SYLVETTE

A Chat with Lydia Sylvette Corbett

"The curators asked her, 'Why no mouth?' She replied airily, 'Oh, I didn't speak much.'"
- Lydia, when viewing her Picasso portraits in San Antonio

Many people have many different views and ideas about Picasso, the man, the artist and the myth. Ask his wives, particularly Francoise Gilot, and you will get a very different portrait to the one his friends or associates might speak of. Quite often, the perception of an individual person is down to the perceiver themselves, and the summarisation might be made up entirely of what traits came forth in your particular relationship with the subject. In the case of Picasso, he was many things to many people; superstar to the world media, genius to his army of admirers, handy PR man for the Communists, complicated man to family and friends. To Lydia Sylvette David, now known by her married name of Lydia Corbett, Picasso was a warm, funny, fun and approachable man, an artist in the truest sense who later inspired her to take up painting herself. She met Picasso when she was 19 in 1953, and as luck would have it, he ended up painting her in a series of legendary art works the following year which have transcended their time. Indeed, Lydia, or Sylvette as the world knows her, has become a myth, a symbol in Picasso folk lore, and as we agreed in our chat, immortalised forever, rather like a goddess out of the mythological tales Picasso so adored.

As with much of Picasso's work, especially his truly great pieces, there is a certain magic to his Sylvette paintings, almost as if they could have been painted at any time in the past, any time in the future, or even on another planet. In the various masterworks, Picasso captures her innocence, her shyness, her unconscious mystery. No question, he is clearly fascinated with her, though his fascination is unique in the Picasso timeline. She was not his lover, though it remains a mystery if he wished to be so or not, and that perhaps explains why the pieces are so flattering. Also, Picasso clearly respected Sylvette; that much is clear from the way he elevates her in the paintings.

She sat for Picasso regularly between April and June and the results were monumental. Her boyfriend Toby came by too, and she has since noted he was not jealous of Pablo's gaze upon his young girlfriend, though many men would have been. Picasso, though, would not start working until her boyfriend left, and then the magic

38

would begin. If Picasso was painting her to forget about his worries after the departure of Francoise, then she was not just a muse, but also a councillor, a silent presence who brightened his days and filled his mind with good thoughts, making him temporarily overlook his heart ache. Though many negative critics have done so, to overlook this work as a stop gap between wives and inspirations is doing the paintings a disservice; after all, they are wonderfully painted, fun even, playful and full of light. Though he did not paint her again and their friendship drifted away when he hooked up with Roque, these paintings deserve classic status, and Lydia needs to be seen as one of the important muses, even though they never shared a romantically intimate moment. It is for this reason perhaps, that Sylvette deserves even more credit. She enjoys an exclusivity in the Picasso story.

The fact that the pictures are not pained, tortured, contorted or emotionally charged ensures that certain people do not take them seriously; which is a shame, as they highlight the more loving, affectionate and positive aspects of Picasso's work. I feel Chrstoph Grunenbcry, director of Kunsthalle Bremen in Germany, who exhibited half the Sylvette works several years ago, hit the nail on the head when he spoke to the BBC in 2014:

"The idea that this series lacks emotional engagement is a rather superficial psychological argument. I don't think you can reduce Picasso to a kind of flesh-eating vampire who feeds on other women and his subjects – it's more complex than that. Maybe it was her resistance to be seduced by him that made him need to see her: because he didn't conquer her, he needed to conquer her on canvas and on paper and in sculpture. But even in the very sketchy portraits, where he tries to capture Sylvette in just a few lines and strokes, there is always great painterly expression. So one has to be very careful not to be judgemental."

Sylvette must have been a hugely important inspiration to the ageing Picasso. He sculpted her, painted her, drew her, and in every piece she is positive, full of life while still being totally still and impenetrable. 'I had this gorgeous hair and, like Coco Chanel," she told the Mail a few years ago. "I used to tailor a man's shirt or jacket to fit me. I was like an iceberg. You couldn't get close to me. They didn't dare come near me, the men. That was why Picasso was intrigued.'

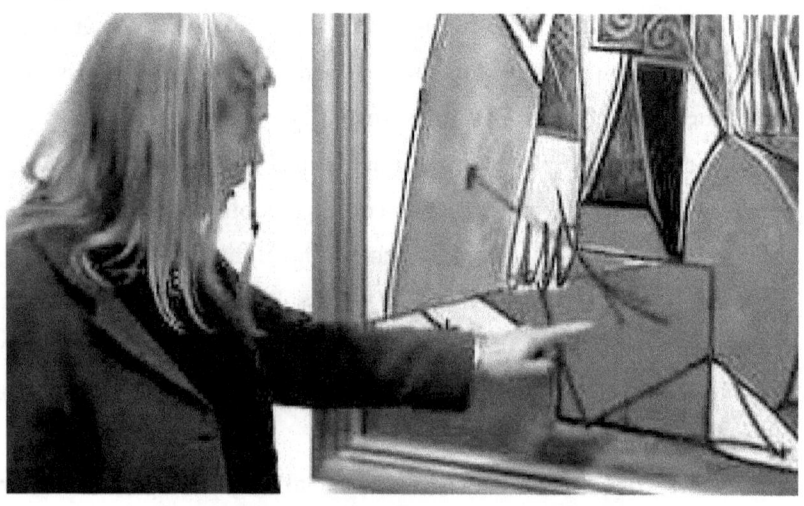

Lydia inspects one of Picasso's portraits of her.

The works were acclaimed upon being unveiled and Lydia became world famous, known as The Girl with the Pony Tail, inspiring the look of Brigitte Bardot, who wanted Picasso to paint her too. He refused of course, for though Bardot was a beautiful and fashionable girl of the time, she was no Sylvette in the eyes of Picasso. She didn't have the innocence, the quiet allure and the mystery.

Writing for Fosse Gallery in 2015, Anthony Sheridan put it beautifully: "Beyond her pale almost translucent skin, Sylvette was flesh and blood; she was bohemian and unconventional. Whilst reserved she was no stranger to love, and she refused to be either "a goddess or a doormat" in Picasso's terms. She was not what Picasso was used to. Sylvette David was not a blank empty presence that he could project on to, that would have been without challenge..."

When she left his studio for the last time, Picasso said to Lydia, "Thank you for being here during my difficult time." Correctly perhaps, Lydia thinks she might have been a healing force between the two women in his life, soothing his pain in a challenging time by being straight forward in her reserved manner. Though she did not accept money, he gifted her with one of the portraits and handed her a book of drawings. One must agree, the painting was a much better gift than a mere pay cheque.

Lydia is 83 at the time of writing. I spoke to her one rainy day in April, 2018, gazing out of the window as she spoke of her first hand encounters with the most iconic artist of the 20th century. As soon as she picked up the phone I felt her warmth and positivity glowing out and heading down the phone line. She entered Picasso's life at a vital time - after the departure of Francoise and the children no less - and some say he found a kind of peace and comfort in the young girl's innocence and hopeful naivety. It must be added that Picasso created more works of Lydia/Sylvette than he did of any other woman in his whole life in one sitting. Certainly, he depicted Jacqueline more in terms of numbers over their twenty year relationship, but Lydia gets

41

the most in one collection. Though some critics sideline these paintings, they are among my personal favourite Picasso works. They are uplifting, classical, timeless, but also mysterious, though they remain pleasing on the eye and seem to say something deep about youth. Lest we forget, Picasso was already in his early seventies when he sat down to paint the young girl before him.

Lydia took me back to that remarkable time in the mid fifties, in the hills above Vallauris, where Picasso had a villa where she encountered him over 60 years ago. Creating is about capturing something in that moment you are present; an essence, a feeling, a quality you cannot bring to life in any other way. Interviewing remarkable people like Lydia is also about capturing an essence of them and their memories. And when she told me about sitting for Picasso, I could almost smell the paint...

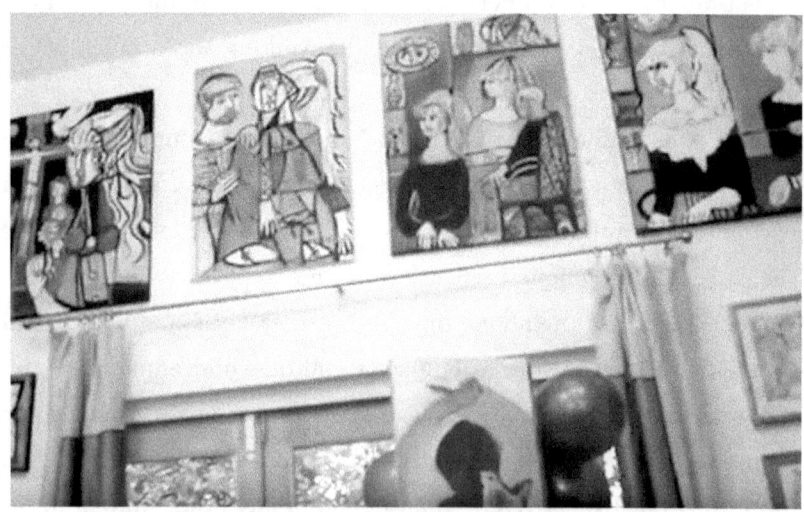

One of the walls in Lydia's home, showcasing her own
Picasso infused artwork.

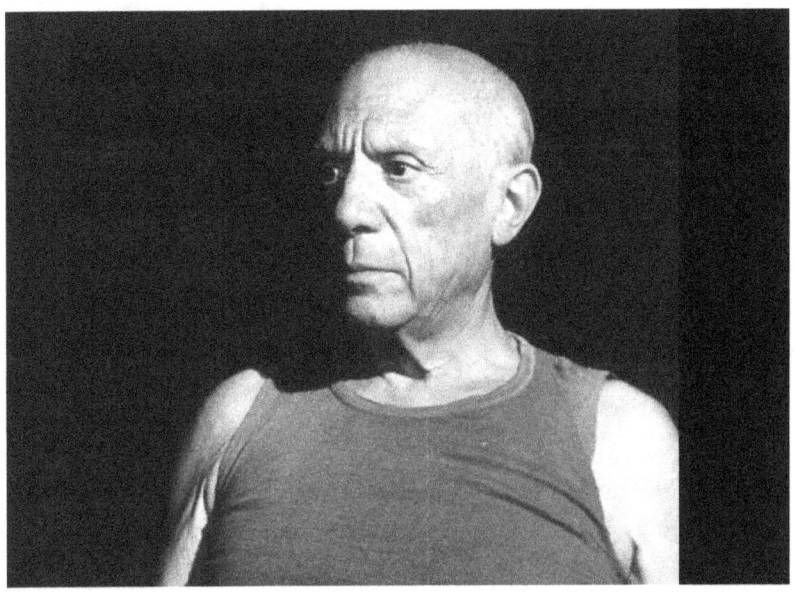

What was it like the first time you met him? He was already a legendary figure, so you must have been aware of his stature. Was it an intimidating meeting or was it more relaxed?

No, it was very relaxed. It was a little village in the south of France. I had a boyfriend who was a metal worker in a little shed. Picasso could see us because he had a studio further up the hill. I think he could see me going there to see Toby, my boyfriend, and he got interested in me. He knew my name, because he must have asked around. And then another day we sat on a terrace; the potteries have a big terrace where they dry the pots in the sun, you know. And I had friends who lived near that pottery, so we all sat on the terrace drinking coffee, smoking away. In those days you could smoke as much as you wanted. Nobody cared.

A bit different now then...

Yes! I loved that. Everybody smoked cigarettes. Anyway... So Picasso saw us. He came over his wall with a sketch of Sylvette, the girl with the pony tail. So that is how it started. He opened a gate and we all rushed into his studio and he said 'I want to paint Sylvette...'

Wow. Amazing really.

Yes and I was so amazed because I was very shy and simple. Not at all exciting. Funnily enough, I was very shy and I had my boyfriend, you know, from England, and so when Picasso said he wanted to paint me I was just amazed. I said yes, I would love it. Because he was very friendly and father like. He was not at all frightening. He was 73. You know, I don't know how old you are...

I'm thirty two.

(Laughter) Oh very young. So it is hard for you to imagine what it is like to be 73.

Yes exactly, my dad is only 64.

Yes so he is quite young too.

That is why I am so fascinated by the idea that you were so young and he was in his seventies when he painted you, and now you are older than he was at the time. He was already a legend by then. I

suppose I am wrapped up in the myth of Picasso, but you were actually physically there.

Well I did not know much about him. I knew he was in the village, you know, and he went to the pottery where he did pots. But I did not speak. I was speechless, because he was a big man. Everybody knew that. I was shy, I did not talk much, but he didn't talk much either. What he did like was my hair, my long neck, and thin body. And I was shy. I think that is what he liked best.

What I like most about the pictures he did of you, is how there seems to be a lot of respect there. It is clear in the paintings.

Yes, you are right! That's it. I think he made me look like a goddess of the Greeks or the Egyptians. Like the Sphinx. Do you know what I mean?

Oh yes, definitely.

So I am really honoured near the end of my life, to have been made into a goddess in a way. (Laughter)

Yeah you have a point. It's like timeless myth really.

Yes, timeless myth, that's right. You know, so he did it and he said it was me. I was amazed.

How many pictures did you sit for?

Well I don't know if I sat for as many as he did, but I think he did more than I sat for. It was very quick, but he made sixty paintings, lots of drawings and sculptures. And the metal sculptures, Toby was cutting some of them out for him. I did not want to be paid as a model, as I was afraid that he would ask me to pose in the nude! (Laughter)

Yes, as soon as he hands the cash over he can pretty much do what he wants then can't he?

Yes, exactly. I thought 'If he asks me to do that I am not doing it.' Anyway, he never dared to ask. He knew I was very not touchable.

Maybe that is what he liked the most, that quality...

Well he did. I was a bit like a child. He loved his children. And they left him. Francoise and the children left him. So that is where I was, in the middle of that sadness. And there was another woman in the pottery, Jacqueline Roque, so I was kind of in the middle of all that.

You kind of arrived at a vital time didn't you?

Yes definitely, to cheer him up really, to make him forget about his troubles. An artist, you know, goes into another world. I am an artist now too, and I go into another world. I do not think about the problems of life, I really don't. I go to a peaceful state, dream-like. Life is great that way, total peace. You're creative too, you know that.

Certainly. It must be strange to look back on the Picasso connection, to be this kind of iconic symbol.

Well I am honoured. It is an honour. Thank God for everything, and now I am doing a big art show of my own, three rooms of my art in London. I do more oils than water colours now, because my eye sight is not so good. Creativity is the key to happiness. You agree don't you?

I do, definitely. It's also like an addiction. But Picasso must have influenced your art. It is there in your paintings for sure, the spirit of Picasso...

Oh, he has inspired my art a lot. A lot! It is all in my work now. I can see the influence. I loved the way he drew lines so quick, and clear, you know? Marvellous drawings. I do the same, a bit. Well, I try to. I am not as good as him! Picasso liked mythology; he loved the Greeks and all those people. He liked all those stories. Me not so much, I am more into spirituality, the spiritual world, I love God and Jesus, and all religions.

So faith and creativity keep you so positive as the years go by. You are still active even now you are in your eighties. And it's remarkable that in his seventies, Picasso was still as creative as ever before too.

Yes. I was there in 1954, and of course he died in 1973. I had two babies by then. Unfortunately I did not really stay in touch with him after. I saw him last in 1965 with my eldest daughter. I remember my daughter swinging him round in a chair. But he moved on with his wife Jacqueline and he was getting old.

I'm interested to know what it was like to have those famous black eyes staring at you while he painted you. I know he was not intense with you personally, but it must have been amazing to watch him studying you like that.

Oh no, he was not intense with me. He looked at me and maybe, I don't know, maybe wondered about me; what is she doing, what is she thinking and what will she do later? Because I was quiet and shy. I spoke about it all with my daughter, I spoke into a little machine and she recorded me, and it was quite emotional, you know.

Does that often feel like a different life to you, almost like a different person?

Yes, because when you are 83 you are not 19 anymore, but you know, young people, they do not think that far away do they? They do not see the future. They live day by day... that's how I lived. Thirty is a nice age, but fifty is better. You have that to look forward to!

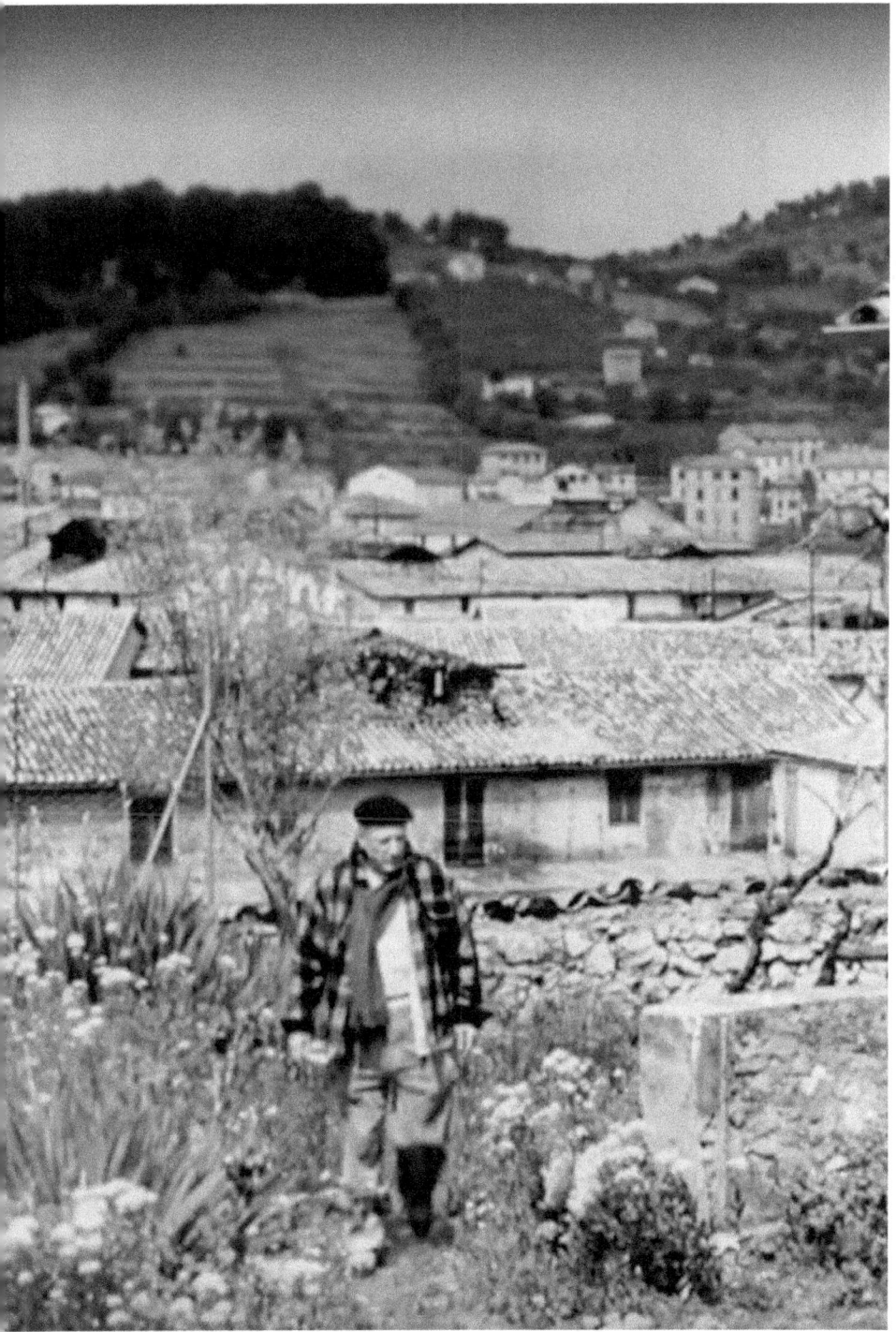

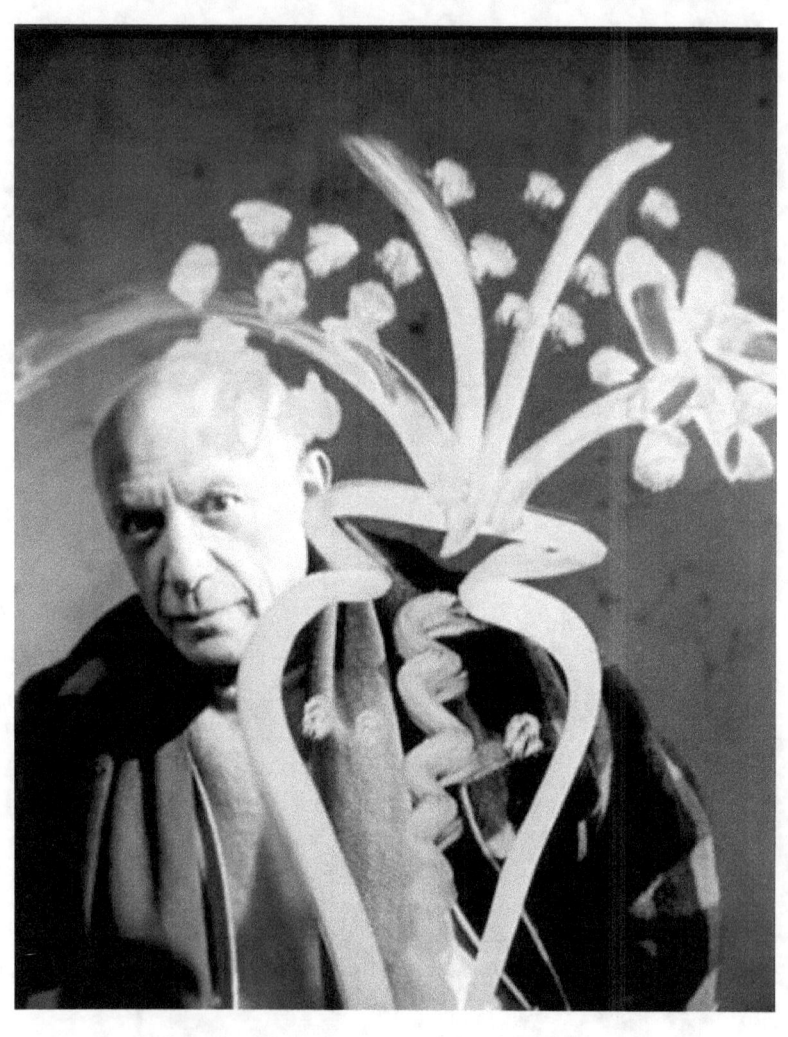

The artist in motion, in a shot from Visit to Picasso (1950).

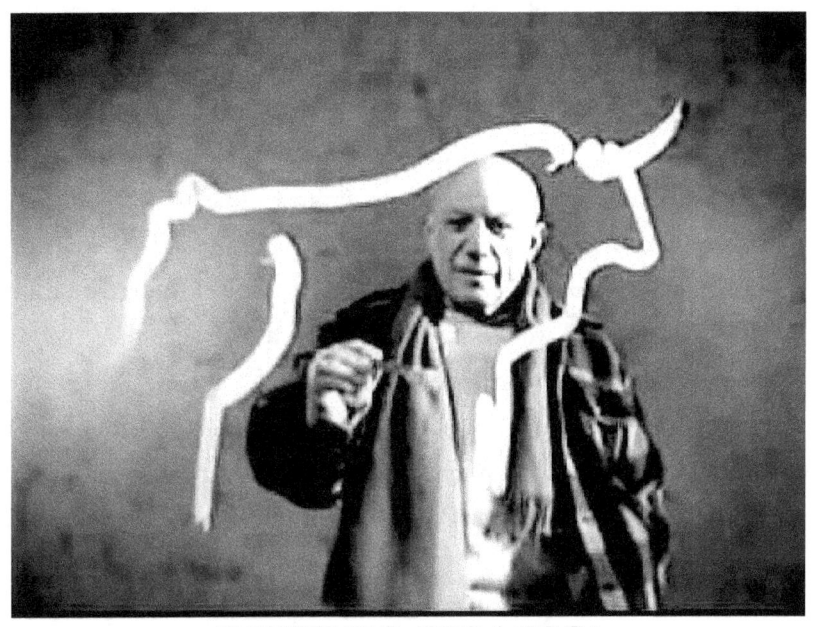

"VISIT TO PICASSO"

Capturing the Essence Of A Genius

Though undoubtedly the work speaks for itself and tells us many essential details we need to know about Picasso the man and Picasso the artist, rare and insightful visual documents reveal something else entirely, something not apparent in biographies or even in the many paintings. There isn't any footage of the young Picasso of course, with moving pictures still being in their infancy when Pablo was youthful, but we are lucky enough to have a fair amount of the older artist on celluloid in various ages and situations. The one main thing that sticks out from such footage are those eyes, black as the night and piercing everything within sight; staring whatever is before him down to nothing, including the camera. A Visit to Picasso, directed by

Paul Haesaerts in 1950, is one such piece of celluloid, capturing the magic of the art and the mystery of the man.

The film begins with a plain opening credit sequence, albeit one soundtracked by sharp, jagged, slightly eerie music (by Andre Souris and Pierre Froidebise), before taking us head first into the Picasso myth, the world of a formidable icon. The camera zooms in on posters of exhibitions, which are adorned by some of the artist's most familiar styles. Then we see a table, on which sit stacks of books on Picasso, a whole library devoted to the painter of his time, illustrating quite literally that he was a legend in his own life time. Frank Silvera's slightly awed commentary brings things together, a typical voice over of the day which sets up this profile beautifully and with honest simplicity. "Picasso," he begins, "a name which challenges and fascinates anyone who cares for the art of painting." The panoramic view of the literary tomes dedicated to the man does linger on for some time, but it does so surely to highlight the fact that more books had been written about Picasso in three decades than had been written on Michelangelo in three centuries.

Silvera then goes on to explain Picasso's urge and drive to reinvent and set new rules, while a faceless man leafs through the books, stopping at key works which were already immortal pieces when the film was made. We are taken back to 1895 when the young Picasso sharpens his skills and begins to combine realism with a personal perspective. Shots of his early 20th century pieces highlight his similarities, at least in this era, to Toulouse Lautrec and Degas, but the film is quick to establish the fact that Picasso went on to carve his own style; though they skip the Blue Period (which is an essential phase), they skim over the Rose Period, the African influences, the arrival of Cubism, the return to Classicalism, and then the return to an abstract/surrealist nature. "An immediate statement" is Picasso's main concern, and by coasting through fifty years of art so speedily, one can see Picasso's extraordinary journey, though harshly depicted, right before your eyes.

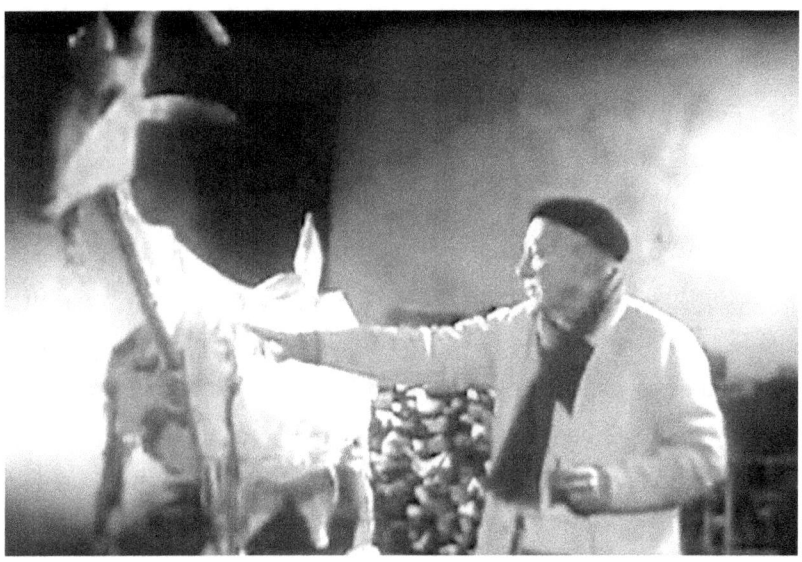

Picasso with one of his sculptures in Visit to Picasso (1950).

Ending its opening lecture on the beautiful drawing of Francoise from 1947, the film then leaves the rigidity of stillness so certain in artwork and takes us into the exciting world of the man himself, the Spaniard living on French soil. We see vintage shots of the village of Vallauris, the place Picasso called home, and then our first glimpse of the man himself, pottering around (no pun intended) his domain, hatted, wearing a thick coat and looking every bit the confident artist happy with his legacy but keen on expanding it. He heads around the corner to his studio, an unassuming barn, where inside he begins to

53

arrange his paintings against a wall. He swivels a wonderful sculpture of a goat, gazing at it lovingly as if it were a child, but also touching it like he might a woman. Though an arranged movement for the camera, orchestrated before the director, you can definitely decipher form these actions alone how Picasso felt about his art works. They were like his children, and he cared for them as such; but he also seems to love them, perhaps desire them, like the females he so needed but rarely understood.

The scene of Picasso revolving the sculpture merges into a beautiful drawing of a goat, a study if you like, and the camera longingly zooms in and out, merging back into the footage of Picasso with the sculpture; haunting, ghostly, slightly unnerving. Pablo then holds up another sculpted masterpiece, like a king raising his sceptre, his shadow cast beautifully on the wall behind him. Wonderfully shot, Picasso then sits before a sculpture of an owl, again, which he turns for the pleasure of the camera. A close up reveals a studious face which turns to a smile, and there is a childlike wonderment when he holds up the small bird piece. Indeed, childlike seems to be the key phrase, for Picasso radiates a naive quality, even if he was anything but naive under the surface. Here he is playing Picasso the curious artist, the thinker, the impulsive creator, the man-child let loose in his artistic life.

Then comes what is certainly the most famous sequence in the film, with Picasso, wearing coat and scarf, painting familiar, iconic emblems on to glass; the bird firstly, which is simplistic but impactful. There is a look of glee on his face, but the shot cuts harshly to a stark drawing of a bull and the soundtrack changes its tone from gentle playfulness to forbidding doom. Picasso then, on a sheet of glass which separates us physically from the artist but not visually, begins to draw the bull. Picasso was addicted to the lure of the bullfight, and saw himself as a mythical blend of bull and man, the Minotaur itself. There is a knowing smile on his face as he sketches the bull, simply and without frills, its dashes and splatters doing more than any precise, exact, photo-like painting ever could. Right on cue, out come various Picasso bull drawings and sketches, an animal he clearly adored. And as with the women he knew, he totally deconstructs and reconstructs the proud beast, the one whose destiny is death; granted it's an honourable death, but death all the same. It is a reverse study, starting with the full bodied bull and ending up as a skeletal frame, breaking the creature down to its bare essentials.

Picasso continues to playfully draw on the glass, next going to the clichéd favourite for many an artist in study - the vase of flowers. There is a wonderful moment of mischief when Picasso stops painting for a moment, bends down and peers at the camera lens through a gap in the flowers. For that one moment, you feel like Picasso is staring right at you; not just the camera, but *you* as you sit there, decades later. It's both funny and rather haunting, for his black eyes seem too vivid, too real, too penetrating to be merely on film. They gaze, they stare, they judge, just like the subjects of many his paintings; the nude whores, the ghost like self portraits and the deformed females.

As the soundtrack becomes more magical - almost carnival like - Picasso paints a horned figure in the centre of the glass, and bending over, pokes his face between the bosoms, giving the camera a knowing glance. He goes off to a doorway and paints the glass that sits in the frame, this one a leggy, slender female, and he does so boldly, quickly and without hesitation. We are seeing a master at work, though he is certainly playing up to the public's perception of himself; Picasso the lover, the ladies man, the bull, the Minotaur, the childlike artist, the spontaneous creator.

We are then shown the Picasso museum, the vast spaces dedicated entirely to his drawings, paintings and pottery. Once inside, one feels the overpowering joy of his work, the passion, and his loves which he cemented forever in these immortal pieces. They are stunning, and presented in black and white as they are, with dream like music on the soundtrack, only enhances the mythical quality of Pablo and his world. The Man With the Sheep, a breathtaking sculpture, takes centre stage and stands as a monument to the man himself. The breathtaking awe which his work inspires has rarely been captured as well as it is here. Documentaries may delve into the private Picasso and roam the places he called home, socialised in or merely roamed, but few of those films elevate the work as it so deserves. Haesaerts, intent only on capturing the myth, magic and artistry of this genius, and not the man behind the wonderment, succeeds in glorifying the creator and his heavenly creations. As the narrator says, these works sum up the "joy and gaiety of living, as well as despair and destruction." No work which came before or after Picasso's could have hoped to come close to how he summed up what it is to be alive and human, with flaws and all.

To creepy sounds, Picasso stands in a black room, painting shapes on the vast glass wall before him, revealing to us what it must be like being the canvas and looking out at the painter; the canvas beginning its life blank, clean and virginal before the artist begins weaving his magic. The brush strokes are thick, broad, yet very careful too, and applied with love. This sequence, with nothing but gothic organ music playing in the background, highlights the vital importance of Picasso's lines, his technique, and the passion which he put into all his work, however "great" or "inconsequential" it might be considered. There is a sense of liberation here, and Picasso applies the paint with joy, the man, the woman and the goat naked, free and full of life. Picasso is nearly seventy in this footage, but seems ageless, timeless, and sort of immortal somehow.

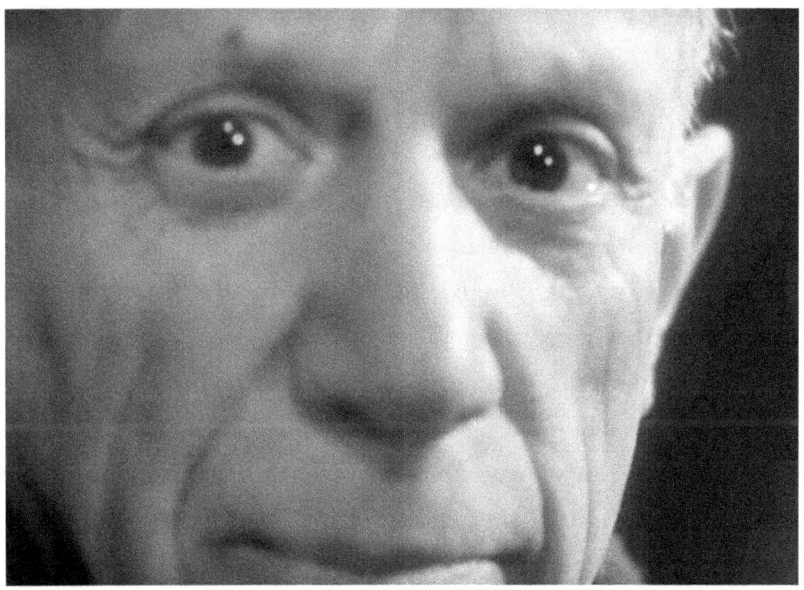

Intensity personified. Picasso at the end of Visit to Picasso (1950).

The film ends with a series of shots of some of his mightiest work, including a longing exploration of every corner of his masterpiece Guernica, reflecting the horror of war with terrifying organ music. The shot of this iconic, everlasting work blends into a close up on the man himself, intense eyes as he smokes his cigarette, and sees us off by signing his name on a white surface. He signs "Picasso, Vallauris, 1950" somewhat enigmatically. The film ends.

Visit to Picasso is not the most well known Picasso visual document, but it certainly stands up to the more famous Mystery of Picasso, shot and released six years later. It is simple, straight forward, unpretentious, and captures the vitality and what looks like Picasso's effortless brilliance. As art films go, it is certainly up there with the best. Comparing to similar film portraits of artists, its lack of frilliness holds it up as a bold, brave and also rather stark look at the creative process, the impatient urgency and importance of free expression captured on celluloid. Salvador Dali's Soft Self Portrait, a film which explored his life and art on the coast of Cadaques twenty years later, could not have been more different. Though it did capture Dali at work (and indeed, rather aptly, painting on a clear surface in a manner similar to Picasso, though surrounded by sycophants and hippy hangers on), it was mostly about theatrics, performance and the illusion of being the surreal court jester Dali had become at that point. Visit to Picasso then, in comparison, is less staged, even if Picasso plays up to his well documented intensity with long, cold, dark stares into the camera. Compared to Dali's film however, Picasso's could not be more truthful, more real or more raw. It captures the simplicity of his art, and the fact that being an artist really is like being a child. As Picasso said, we are all born artists; it's just remaining one which becomes the big challenge. Judging by the way Picasso jots, paints and sketches to his fancy, roaming the vast spaces of his studio and admiring his own primitive sculptures, Picasso pretty much lived the life of a creative and unrestricted man, his eyes full of excitement as if discovering new sensations every moment where nothing was off limits to his endlessly dazzling, restless imagination. This film seems to contain essential elements of what made Picasso a magician of art, somehow bottling up a fragment of his soul, forever on film for future generations to study, dismiss or celebrate. It offers no insight into his life, his psychology, his psyche or approach to life and the challenges it presents to us on a daily basis, merely providing proof that Picasso, the mythical being, actually existed in the flesh. Hearing his name as a child for me summoned up feelings of awe, and to me he was a being from another age who achieved genius time and time again; a man whose work could not be understood completely because it was so full of varied ideas, changing styles and adult themes I could not grasp at the time. As one grows and is faced again with the staggering footage in Visit to Picasso, the mystery begins to unravel, the clear glass being symbolic of how simple it is to understand Picasso's primal urges. Picasso wanted the artist's life from when he was a toddler. Here, approaching seventy, the fact he got to keep that dream alive, no matter what was happening behind closed doors in his private life, is truly remarkable. Visit to Picasso remains an invaluable glimpse into the life of a genius.

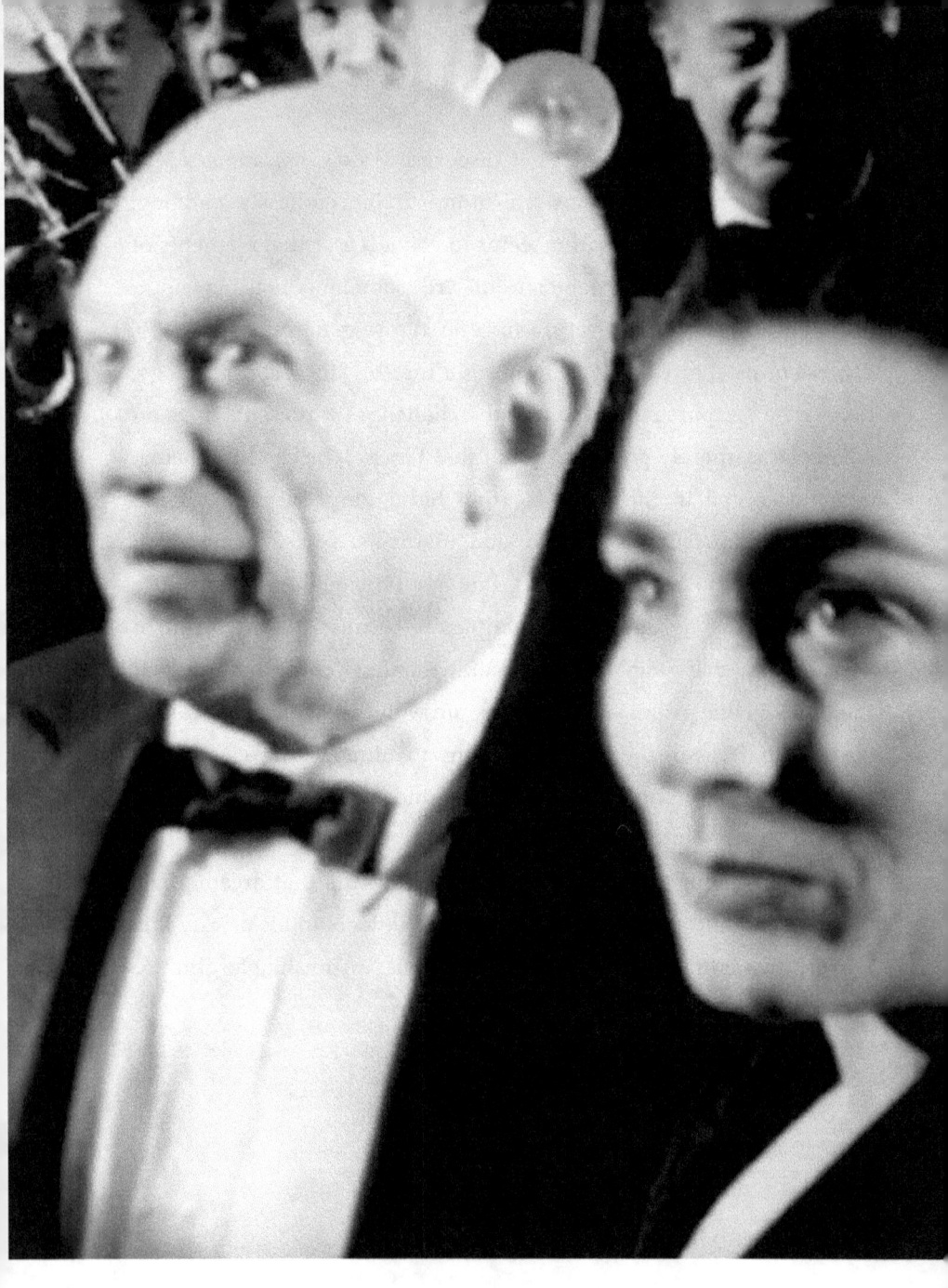

Picasso and Jacqueline before the world's press.

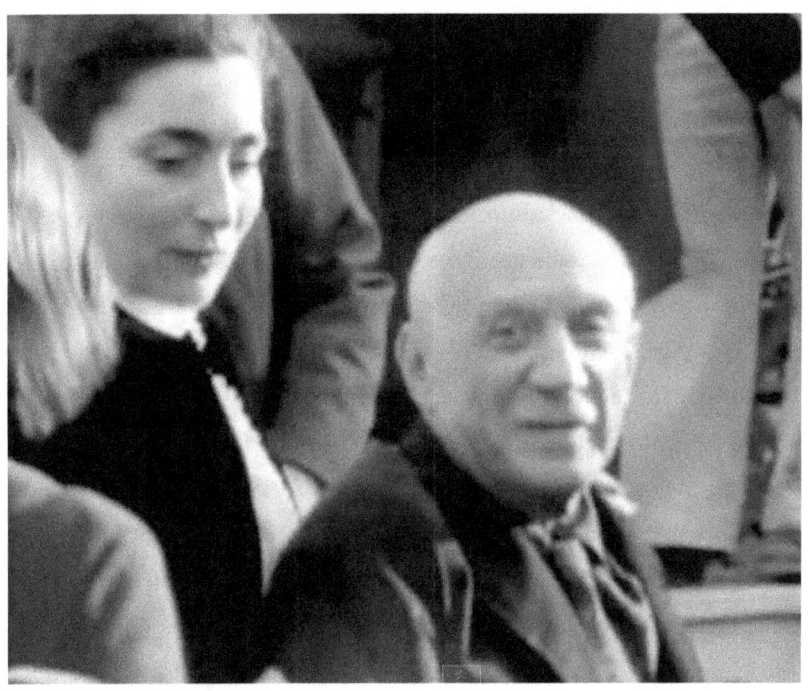

WHEN PABLO MET JACQUELINE

Art's Great Romance

The post-Francoise Picasso of 53 and 54 cuts a very sorry figure; an aging ladies' man no longer able to control his women; a man doubting his vitality as death becomes an ever more present concern. Though destructive, the end of Francoise and Pablo's union was unfortunate, for he had not just lost his muse and lover, but also his two children, Paloma and Claude, who he adored, and were now no longer close by. In the aftermath of her exit, he was enraged, furious and bitter, but when he finally stopped complaining to friends and hangers on, he began to work again at a furious rate. In the works were Francoise, the approaching silhouette of death, and his tragically waning power. He ridiculed himself and depicted the light in which Francoise now viewed him - as a dirty old man, essentially.

Still, over the horizon, was a glimmer of hope. Jacqueline Roque was working at the Madoura Pottery. When Picasso was there the two would speak and share laughter. His nickname for this beautiful girl was Madame Z. She had the dark looks of Francoise but was much smaller, two inches shorter than Picasso in fact, which seemed important some how. She had been married to an engineer called Andre Hutin, and lived in Africa as Jacqueline Hutin where they had a young daughter, Catherine. She moved to France, divorced Andre and returned to her maiden name. So like Picasso, she had a past, though Pablo probably didn't like hearing of hers. She was 26, he was 72. But that did not stop him. Realising he was developing feelings for Jacqueline, he drew a dove on the wall of her home. The dove, thanks to Picasso of course, had become the symbol of peace, but to him at this moment it was just a declaration of romantic interest. As was the single rose he brought to her one day. Though they had met in 1953, they did not begin their romance until 1955, after which time Jacqueline was sure of dating the (much) older man.

Around this time, Picasso was involved with many women, and even had another brush with his old muse Dora Maar, telling her that there was no woman in his life at the moment, perhaps in hope that the two of them could reconnect. The last time Picasso saw Dora was at a social gathering, where he told her there were things he needed to say to her away from everyone. He asked her to stand up and come with him. The friends watched in wonderment, in awe of the iconic couple reunited, and were excited about what was going to happen next. Picasso walked her over to the other end of the room, left her there and returned to his table. It was the last time they ever saw one another. Not the best of goodbyes...

Jacqueline Roque inspired Picasso early on, and she was appearing in his work as early as 1954. He gives her a certain grace, a class of her own, with that exaggerated neck and cat like dignity. Rather like his depictions of Sylvette in 1954, there is indeed a sense of utter most respect for the young Jacqueline in these early pieces, a straight forward but deep admiration, and not yet have any complicated deconstructions begun to seep into the decorative portraits.

Despite the fact he was definitely seeing Jacqueline more often, he still seemed to pine for Francoise, and maybe hoped he could re-spark their romance. The big moment came when Picasso was invited to attend the first bullfight in Vallauris. He had with him an entourage, his children Maya (to Marie-Therese), Paulo (to his first wife Olga), Paloma and Claude, and urged Francoise to accompany him. "You deserve to leave my life with the honours of war," he told her. Francoise agreed to attend, and even open the bullfight on horseback in a symbolic manner fitting to their strange situation. Jacqueline, now a constant presence in Picasso's life, though often in the background saying very little or having very little said to her, objected to this. She said she was hurt, humiliated even by the very idea of it, and urged Picasso to reconsider. When he would not budge, Jacqueline gave in and accepted. "You're right," she concluded. It was a landmark moment, when it was clear to Picasso, herself and everyone else around, that Jacqueline would dedicate her life fully to Picasso.

Surreally, Francoise performed the theatrics out in the bull ring while Picasso sat with his friends, children and, of course, Jacqueline. Pablo praised her efforts and complimented her on her performance. She left him for good that night, and even though he might not have admitted so, he most certainly admired her will power and head strong defiance. With Francoise gone, Jacqueline was now in line to take her place as the woman by his side, the trophy wife hanging on his arm at all times.

Less is written of Jacqueline than Picasso's other long standing partners, and to think he was with her for the final twenty or so years to the end of his life, this is rather strange. Is it because she was the perfect good wife? Is it because she was not a formidable character in her own right, that she was happy to please Picasso and did not require independence? Perhaps so. After all, most people want to hear of turbulent relationships in art, especially if both of them are thinking artists; i.e. Picasso and Francoise, Picasso and Dora. But with Jacqueline it was something different all together, and from the outside one might think he found the ideal wife in the last chapter of his life, a loyal rock out for his best interests.

That's not to say the transition from Francoise to Jacqueline was smooth and instant. There were, of course, other women in between. Picasso took time looking for the chosen one, the female to embody and make reality of all his fantasies and requirements. "Whores for daddy" Paulo said of the other women, while Maya admitted that though they were getting younger and younger, she could have fun and accepted them all as possible stepmothers. Paule de Lazerme, an associate at the time, said Jacqueline was watching close by intently, "eager to fill the vacant place." As time went on, Picasso realised

Jacqueline was the perfect woman for him, especially when Francoise told him that she was getting remarried. "I hope it's a fiasco, you ungrateful creature" were his final words on the matter apparently.

Picasso painted numerous pieces of Jacqueline over the next two decades, more than anyone else in his life for that matter (though his biggest ever series on one person were his works on Sylvette in 1954), meaning of course that in many ways he had found his ultimate muse. When Matisse died in 1954, Picasso was deflated by the passing of a long time friend and rival, and his reaction was to immediately paint Jacqueline in Turkish costume. She went on to inspire his series of Delacroix variations, given that Jacqueline reminded Picasso of one of the women in the legendary Women of Algiers piece. Indeed she had an elegant classicalism about her, which must have pleased Picasso no end, ever the one to obsess and idolise the Old Masters and their perfect female figures.

Perhaps the strongest image of her in the Picasso canon though, arguably at least, is the very first. Jacqueline With Flowers was painted in 1954, and bears many similarities to his Sylvette works, in that there is a Sphinx-like quality to her, with the long neck, bright colours and serious, bewitching eyes. As you can tell by the portrait, Picasso thought she had the classic look about her, a muse fitting for a genius, and he wasted no time drawing these qualities out.

And so they set out on their path together, living in his vast home, La Californie, the mansion Picasso bought in 1955. He had left Vallauris behind, and was about to begin the next phase of his life.

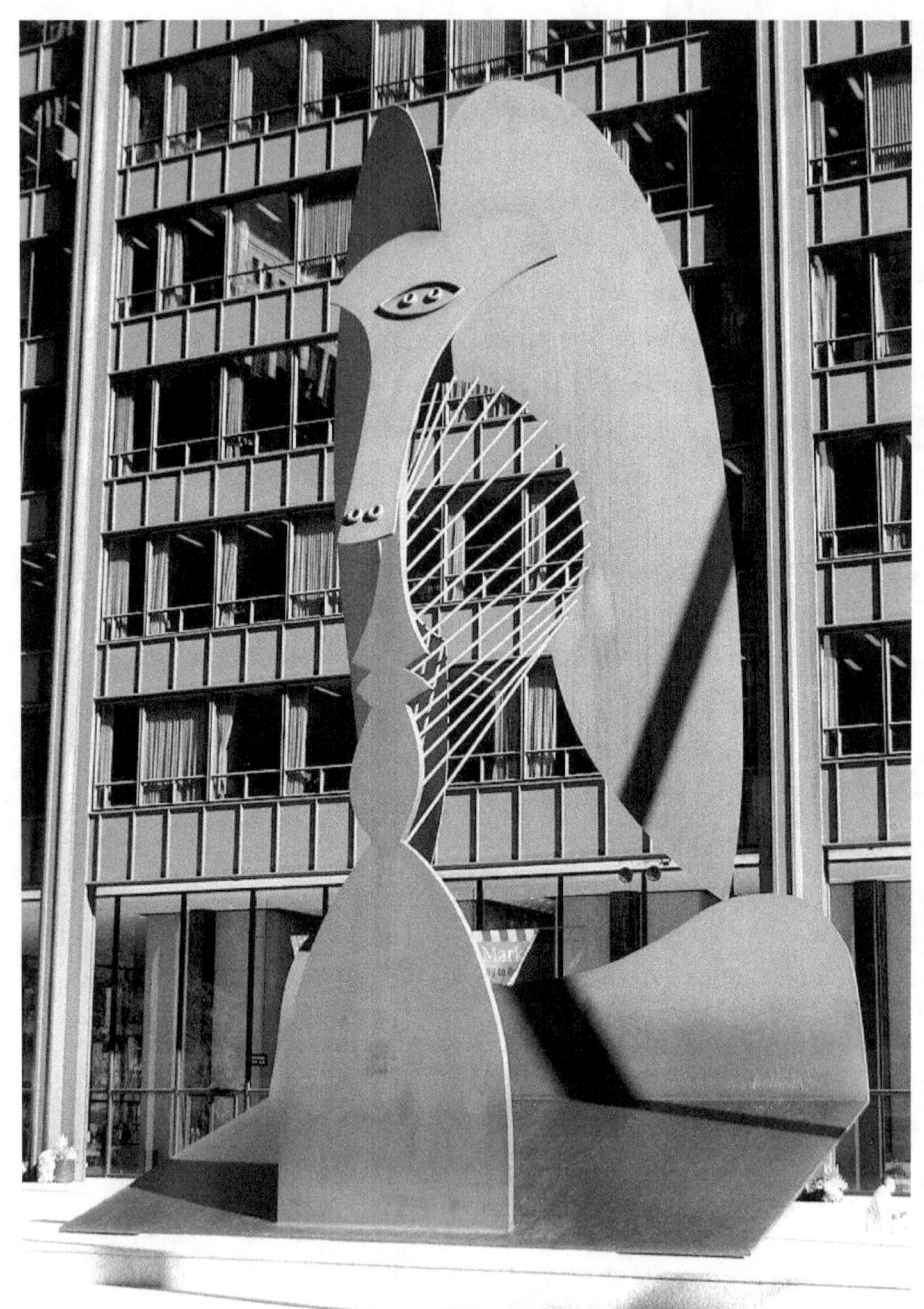

Picasso's sculpture in Chicago.

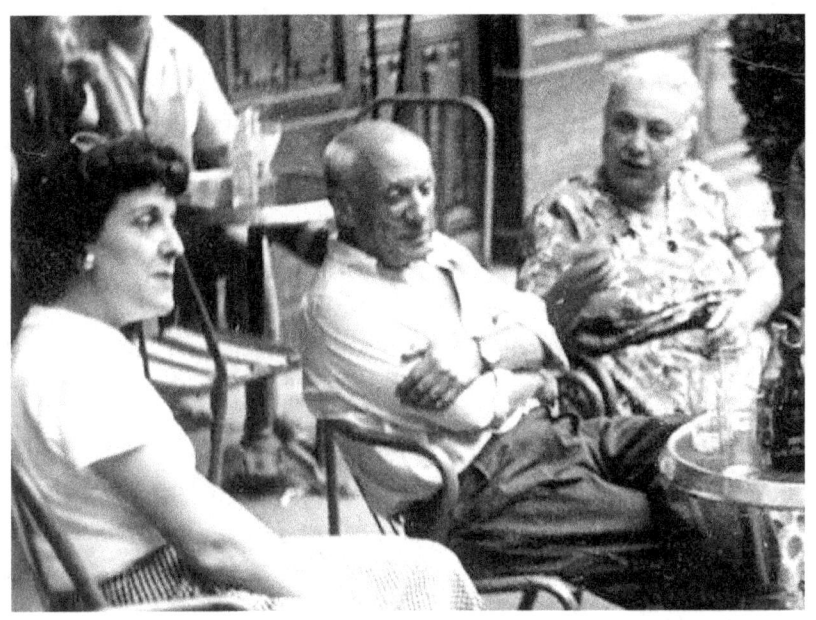

PAST, PRESENT AND FUTURE

Picasso: Man of the People in the 1950s

"Success is dangerous. One starts to copy oneself and copying oneself
is more dangerous than copying others. This leads to sterility."
-Picasso, 1956

The fifties, though many people might disagree, were one of the
most important decades in Picasso's career. In this time frame he saw
the departure of Francoise, the arrival of a new woman, Jacqueline,
the reminder he was mortal, while also creating several works which
though often sidelined by critics are among his most interesting
artistic statements from the second half of his life. These were not the
"triumphant years" as John Richardson might call them, but from the

1950s onwards Picasso became more human, frailer in some ways, ever aware of his mortality, therefore more relatable. It's there in the work, the feeling that the Picasso power is dimming ever so slightly, even if he remained just as defiant and sure of himself on the exterior to the prying eyes of the globe.

Fifty plus years into his life as a serious artist, Picasso was still only interested in his own presentation and idea of an object, a subject, colour or vision. Though rich and famous, his views had changed very little and he was not a sell out. He remained a good Communist (he had joined the party in 1944), a man driven by his art and uncorrupted by the wealth that had come his way. The hobnobbing, smartly dressed socialite he had become when living with Olga back in the 1920s was long gone, and the ageing bohemian reigned supreme. His views on art and expression had remained true and firm, and he saw art as a singular force of expression, the beauty of it depending on where you are standing, but the validity based on the eye of the creator first and foremost.

"The colour red and those apples and oranges or that bottle of water or that bottle of wine," he said in 1957, "that is my guitar. It may not be yours. It may not be Jacqueline's. But it's mine. You see, we go to the Beaux-Arts. They try to teach us everything. They wind up by teaching us nothing. They have us make copies of everybody, trying to turn us into another Velasquez or another Goya or maybe Poussin, and we remain nobody. Art begins with the individual. When the individuality appears, that's the beginning of art. So much for my guitar. The trouble is, we've been taught what to see and how to render what we see. If we could only be in the position of the men who did those wonderful drawings in the caves at Lascaux and

Altamira! They had nothing to go by, nothing to build on. They had to start from scratch. Well, we can't, of course. That was the Golden Age and we can't dream of bringing it back. So we have to resort to all kinds of intellectual devices to re-establish the vigour and validity of our vision. That's the guitar again."

And for Picasso, it was still not about what the viewer thought or failed to understand. "I don't paint pictures in the hope that people will understand them," he said. "They understand or not, according to their capacity. It's wrong to be so concerned about people's understanding, anyway."

In his pottery and sculpting, Picasso's work was anything but mysterious and indecipherable, for the objects resembled exactly what they were, even if they were often made out of household objects, scrap metal, bits and pieces others thought were nothing but rubbish. Picasso literally made a world out of nothing, and looking at his beautiful real life objects, especially those created in the early 1950s, makes you realise how he not only redefined paint, he did the same with sculpture too. He did not have to explain his aims.

Nanny Goat, from 1950 (featured in Visit to Picasso), is one of his most iconic physical works, alongside his similarly striking Man With A Goat, which Picasso considered one of his masterpieces. The Nanny Goat, and the other goat sculptures from this time, presents to us a life long infatuation with the animal made into an eternal object, revealing the personal qualities of his work. Famously, Francoise had gotten rid of his first pet goat when she could not bare the smell, giving it away to gypsies. Fittingly for the woman who would do anything for him, Jacqueline got him another goat as a gift, which he lovingly named Esmeralda. She did not mind the smell so much.

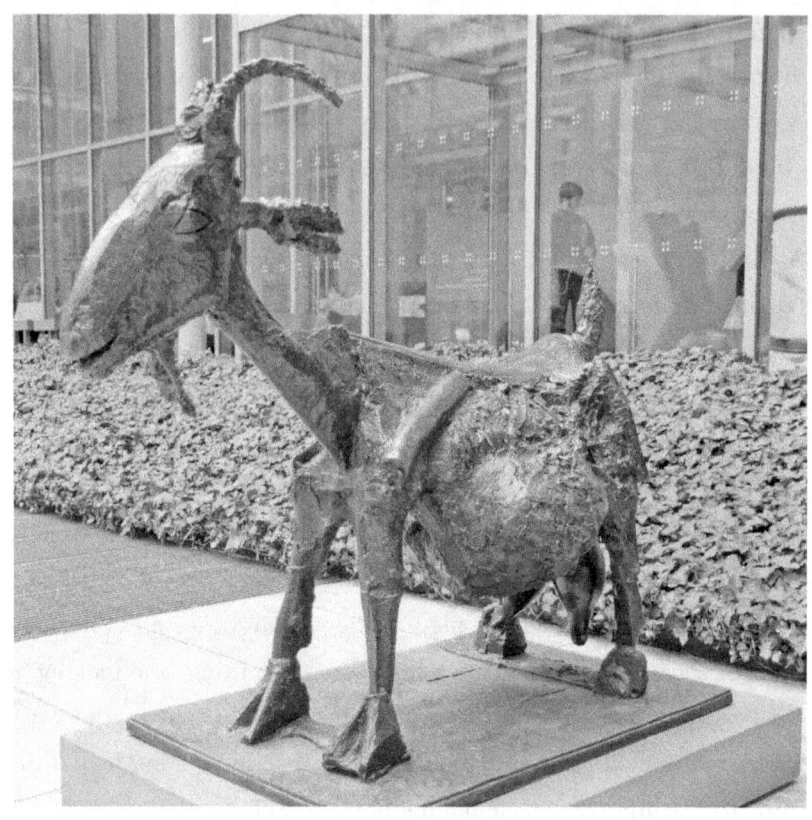

Picasso's She-Goat.

The goat is not just an animal made three dimensional for the sake of it. Like the bull, it was an important part of Picasso's psyche; and besides, it had been around in art since the classical times. The She Goat, also done in 1950, is pregnant, highlighting the positive vibes in Picasso's life in that year. After all, Francoise herself had just had their second child, Paloma, and the joy he felt is evident here in the proud beast. The imminent arrival of a newborn goat also reflects

Picasso's hopes for the coming decade as he approaches seventy. Fertility, a new life, a new dawn...

Animals aside, Picasso was also focused on his family for artistic flavours, and they directly inspired many art works in the early 1950s. A portrait of family bliss is evident in the last few years with Francoise, in particular his beautiful 1950 painting of Francois drawing with the children around her, all moody greys and the odd area of subtle brown. The same mood is evident in Paloma and Claude, done in the same year, although harbouring a little more exotic mystery in its shades.

As Francoise shifted out of his life, she also naturally drifted out of the art. Jacqueline entered the picture, literally, and in a big way too. She begins life in Picasso's work as a classical figure, like one of the women in the works of Delacroix. He transforms the short dark beauty into an exotic, long necked mythical goddess, rather like he did with the young Sylvette in 1954. Jacqueline becomes his new queen, glorified in the work, held up as an example to all females.

In 1954, Picasso captured something almost heavenly about Jacqueline in both of the flower portraits and the crossed hands piece, both timeless pictures preserving her as a mythical being. He also gives her a blue tinge in another self portrait, which reminds one of Picasso's own self portrait fifty years earlier, bearded, morose and dark eyed during the turn of the century in his own Blue Period. She is not yet the sole muse however, for Sylvette takes up more canvases that year; but Jacqueline is creeping in, slowly, and Picasso is more than aware of her beauty. He is vaguely bewitched by her, and becomes more so in the next couple of years.

Come 1955 and Jacqueline is inspiring him in all kinds of ways. She is in Turkish costume again, adorning pottery, naked with cups, and some form of goddess in various works. He seems to relish capturing her dark looks, and portrays her in various guises while retaining her recognisable essence throughout. By 56, Jacqueline dominates the female work, though there are still some sweet portraits of Paloma. Perhaps the most striking Jacqueline piece from 56 is the moody one of her sitting in the studio, a canvas by her side, her hands clasped together, her eyes closed either in slumber or deep thought. It's a beautiful picture, rarely held up as a key work, but one which immediately speaks to the observer. He painted a more colourful version of the same picture, but it was more familiar Picasso fare, and nowhere near as inspired.

In 1959, Jacqueline was captured wonderfully in the series of profile portraits, her essence evident in the broader, more childlike brush strokes. The best though, for me at least, is the more mysterious and bland Jacqueline de Vauvenargues, where his muse sits, in profile once more, against a black background, with the title of the piece above her head. Clearly, she could be whatever he wanted her to be. Still, one cannot help but feel sad somewhat that the children are mostly absent from the latter part of the fifties, replaced by self referential bullish figures, like 1958's stunning drawing Minotaur (a self portrait in disguise?), the King of the Minotaurs, and Still Life With Head of a Bull. In fact, 1958 appears to have been the year of the bull in Picasso's painting workload. The woman eating half man-half bull was more self aware than ever before, even as he settled down with Jacqueline in their new life.

'I stand for life against death; I stand for peace
against war."

Though primarily concerned with his own creative life, Picasso was
also looking outward too, although many have questioned the peace
related work he did in this era, John Richardson in particular citing
some of it banal. His murals in the Vallauris chapel, created in 51
and 52, still divide many to this day, but I feel these works have their
merits. The peace side of the mural is fabulous, no doubt, and the
harmony depicted here is free, liberated and without any self
consciousness or familiar Picasso trademarks. The lack of clichés is
admirable, and Picasso has not given into predictabilities at all. There
is an atmosphere of harmonious togetherness. The war side, though
obviously more heavy handed due to what it is committed to
depicting, seems more familiar, safer somehow, while the centre
piece to it all, the multi coloured figurines joining hands, is rather
lazy for Picasso, even if it does hammer the point home suitably well.
Picasso was for peace, and when he wanted to express this in art, the
simpler the better. After all, the simplicity is what makes an image
iconic. Few would argue that Picasso's simplistic dove drawing for the
1950 World Congress of Supporters of Peace poster is his best work,
but the image did what it was supposed to, and Picasso achieved his
goal in creating an image that effortlessly stood for peace. He had
painted the famous Dove in January of 1949 and saw the image
adopted for the Paris Peace Congress that year, which Picasso also
attended. As if dominating the art scene wasn't enough, he was now
creating images which the whole world collectively associated with
harmony and understanding.

When Picasso reflected his personal world in art, everyone approved in mass unison; yet some of his more political work was indeed causing harsher reactions than he was used to, such as his drawing of Stalin upon his death in 1953, which was met with disapproval by the Communist party. Though often sidelined as hackneyed and lazy, the almost comic book style graphicness of Massacre in Korea (1950) remains one of his strongest political statements, for me at least. However, Picasso expert John Richardson later wrote "the painting's crude imagery might have demonstrated that if Picasso's psyche was not engaged, the message could work against him." On the contrary, I think the picture is rather powerful.

Through the 1950s, Picasso was living out his own legend, setting up a new life in the grand La Californie with Jacqueline, and though one tries hard not to fall for the myth of the man, it is hard when reading first hand accounts of interactions with the artist in his domain. When Carlton Lake visited Picasso for an interview, a vivid description in The Atlantic was published: "We passed into a large salon. The ceiling was well over fifteen feet high. Facing me, on the other side of the room, were floor-to-ceiling glass doors overlooking a terrace and gardens. The room itself and another, somewhat smaller, to my left, were filled with the same kind of overflowing accumulation of Picasso's work that I had encountered as soon as I crossed the threshold into the hall. It seemed a little bit like playing Ali Baba in modern dress. My eyes were racing from one corner to another trying to take it all in at once. Then I heard Jacqueline say, 'Et voici Picasso.' I turned and, across a distance of perhaps two feet, found myself looking down into Picasso's eyes - as bright and penetrating as ever. He looked vigorous yet relaxed, and a long way

74

from seventy-five. He was wearing saffron-colored duck slacks and a burgundy woolen shirt with a dark-brown sleeveless sweater over it; on his feet, a pair of canvas espadrilles. He led me into the dining room to our right, pulled up a chair for me near the head of the table, then settled his wiry, rugged little frame into a wicker seat beside me. Jacqueline sat down on the other side of him, facing me and completing a kind of semicircle. Picasso lighted a cigarette and looked over at me. 'Well,' he said with a grin, "you've got me. Now what are you going to do with me?'"

During the interview, the subject turned, quite naturally, to Picasso's position on Communism, and Lake seemed certain that Picasso should leave the party. Pablo though, most certainly was not. Carlton reported: "'Look,' he said, 'I'm no politician. I'm not technically proficient in such matters. But Communism stands for certain ideals I believe in. I believe Communism is working toward the realization of those ideals.' He paused ever so briefly and then, before I had a chance to speak, picked up the question that was beginning to formulate itself in my thought. 'You'll ask me, what about Stalin?' he said. 'Well, what about him? You would have said he was no good—but you didn't know that; you only thought it. Well, I thought he was. It turned out that I was wrong. But is that any reason why I should renounce the ideals I believe in? Let's say I were a Catholic and I met a priest who was no good—a worthless type in every sense of the word. He's all the bad things you can think of. Is that any reason why I should give up believing in Christianity? There are all kinds of perfectly authentic stories about the sins of the Church in the Middle Ages. Some of the Popes were horrible creatures. But should I—as a Christian—in view of that, give up my

75

adherence to the ideals I believe in? Eh bien, non! That's right. I have no intention of resigning. Things look bad in Poland and Hungary, I know, but I'm not quitting the Party just for that. I don't say the world can't find the cure for its ills under the capitalist system, but thus far it hasn't made very impressive headway.' He studied me for a brief moment, then said, 'I don't understand why Americans are so concerned about Communism, anyway. Especially, about whether some individual is a Communist or not.'"

In 1956, Picasso turned 75. Jacqueline was the definitive woman for him now, and Francoise was out of the picture all together. Given that Olga had died in 1955, Picasso was now free to marry Jacqueline whenever he felt. Though happy with his new wife-to-be, there was undoubtedly an air of sadness that Pablo and Jacqueline were unable to have a child together. As good a step dad he was to Catherine, Jacqueline was no longer capable of bearing children, which was a pain made worse by the fact that Francoise fell pregnant in 1956 to her latest partner. Still, Picasso's life was functioning properly now, and Jacqueline acted as the "gatekeeper", more than happy to turn anyone away who might distract the master from his restless life. It was time for more work, and as little personal drama as possible.

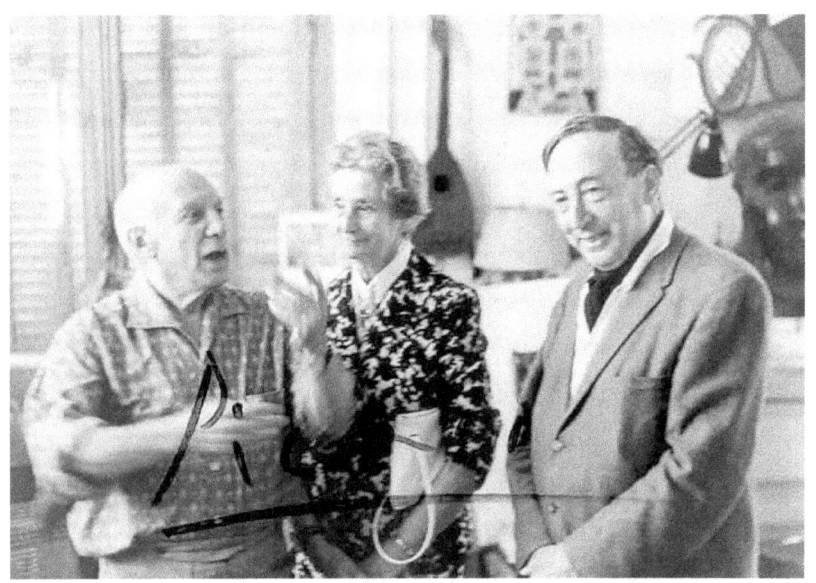

Though Picasso was at his best when painting his own world, however cut off and bubble like it was, he also excelled in reinventing the past he so respected; and not always his own past either, but the classical works of the masters. Nowadays Picasso stands alongside the historical painters without question, but while a living artist his legacy was unfinished, and it was open to debate whether Picasso's work would ever equal that of Valezquez or El Greco. Time has told us, however, that it not only matches it, it surpasses it in influence alone, never mind mass recognition.

At the start of the 1950s, Picasso approached El Greco, incorporating his own style and respectfully bastardising the work his forbearer did in the 16th and 17th century. His portrait of El Greco is staggeringly rich in colour, respecting the rigidity of tradition, but also refusing to give in to it. Picasso had long been an admirer of El Greco, and that is reflected in the warm, loving homage of 1950.

In 1957, he approached the mother of them all and did a huge amount of variations on Las Meninas by Diego Valezquez, the biggest challenge of all to Picasso. To many painters of the time, especially Salvador Dali, Valazquez was one of the true geniuses of painting, held in the same regard as Goya, Raphael and Da Vinci. But Picasso was not interested in aping his style, but redefining it, ensuring the observer viewed it differently but also accepted it as a new form in itself, just as worthy of respect; indeed, as they had earlier with cubism, collage and modern classicalism, not to mention surrealism, which Picasso had no doubt also practiced in his time. But the Valezquez pictures are different. This series became an obsession, and though he was often bad tempered when things were not going his way in the art department, he was especially tormented by this, a challenge considered the Everest of art. If he could not reach this peak, it was effectively over for him. There are accounts of Pablo being up in the studio for days during the tackling of this series, and he was heard banging and clattering around in frustration, believing he was never going to "crack" Valezquez, and that the master would have the better of him. Judging by the results however, it is clear that Picasso reached a goal; and if not *his* goal, then certainly a valid conclusion. There is a mood, a mystery and a lack of colour (greys and blacks, bits of white, variations of all three) which make the reinventions, dare I say so, bolder and richer than the originals. The royal grandness has been replaced by a strangely grounded mystery.

"If someone wants to copy Las Meninas," Picasso said seven years before the series, "entirely in good faith, for example, upon reaching a certain point and if that one was me, I would say... what if you put them a little more to the right or left? I'll try to do it my way, forgetting about Velázquez. The test would surely bring me to modify or change the light because of having changed the position of a character. So, little by little, that would be a detestable Meninas for a traditional painter, but would be my Meninas."

Other artists were inspired to recreate the joys of Valezquez (Dali, Claudio Bravo, John Singer Sargent and Manola Valdes to name but a few), but Picasso's variations remain the most famous and highly respected. But that was not the end of this obsessive urge. In 1959, he embarked on reworking the work of Manet, executing several variations on his key works. It was a time of reinvention, restructure and revival. Though respectful of the past, he was more than happy to deform it and bring it into his own world, mutated and wonderfully recharged by the vibrancy of the 20th century.

He was not just looking to the past in this era, of course. There were new, fresh and grand pieces completed too, work on a more monumental scale. In 1958 he was asked to paint for the UNESCO building in Paris. When asked about what he was going to do for the mural, Picasso was not too sure, though he had more than a few plans. "Oh, I have lots of ideas—they come and they go—but I haven't settled on anything yet," he said teasingly. "I suppose I could do a mural of the Crusaders marching on Constantinople or one showing the august body itself reuniting in plenary session, but what interest would that have for anybody? It would have none for me, I'm sure. Oh, well, I'll hit on something. Subjects are a bore, anyway. I've always said there are no subjects any more."

The results were typically iconic; The Fall of Icarus, a huge work which stands as one of his most memorable and famous from this time. Though one might prefer the more personal pieces, or even the variations on the classics, his Icarus mural remains awe inspiring, grouping the artist in with the myth of Icarus's tale as a fitting metaphor. Granted, it does not come near the impact garnered by Guernica, but that had been an instant reaction to a devastating event. This was a more vague commission, and Picasso used the opportunity to put his stamp on eternity once again, creating the largest work of his career. But the painting retains its mystique and does not go hand in hand with anyone's idea or motives. UNESCO Head of Secretary put it best when he unveiled the new work: "Picasso's panel is a masterpiece and like all masterpieces it cannot be explained. What does it matter what we think of it today? Its beauty will be apparent ten years from now." Indeed, it almost sounded like a statement from Picasso himself.

Picasso saw out the fifties in style, approaching the age of 80 but remaining as active and passionate as ever before. This was a time of looking at the past, trying not to think of the future but being unable to avoid its certainty, and living in the moment, the present, the here and now. The rich Communist was happiest when in his own bubble, but was also happy to express his love of peace, his devotion to its cause and his love for mankind. Though dubbed "a man of doubt", Picasso was as keen as ever to explore, dissect and attempt to defeat the doubt, to understand the complexities of the human soul, the mystery of existence, and the often fatal flaws of man. If he ever got near to the answer is another matter, but Picasso certainly got closer to it than anyone else in the arts, and enjoyed his excursions immensely. The fifties then remain a dichotomy, with Picasso as the artist who experienced turmoil at home but hoped the world outside could go on in harmony.

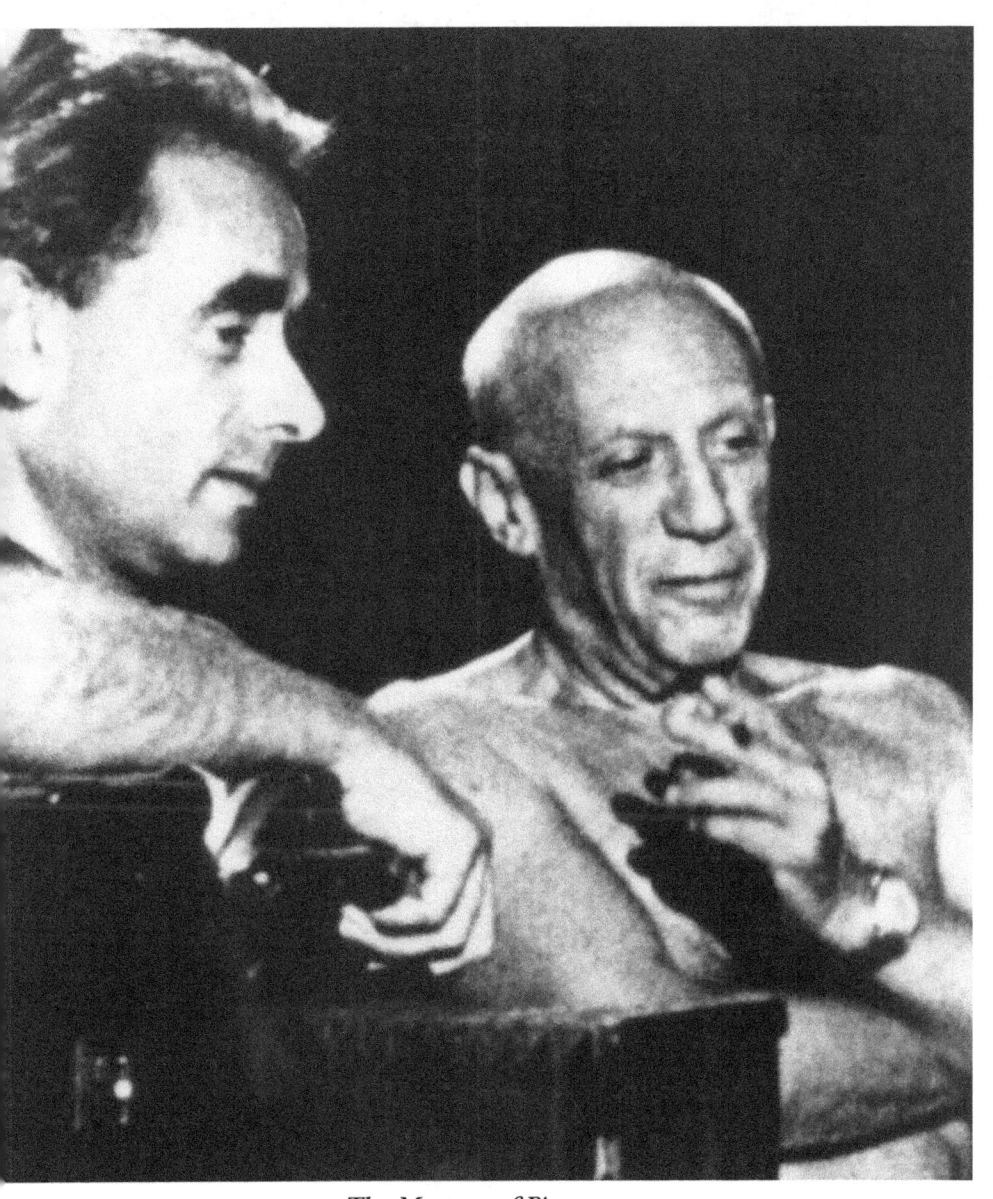

The Mystery of Picasso.

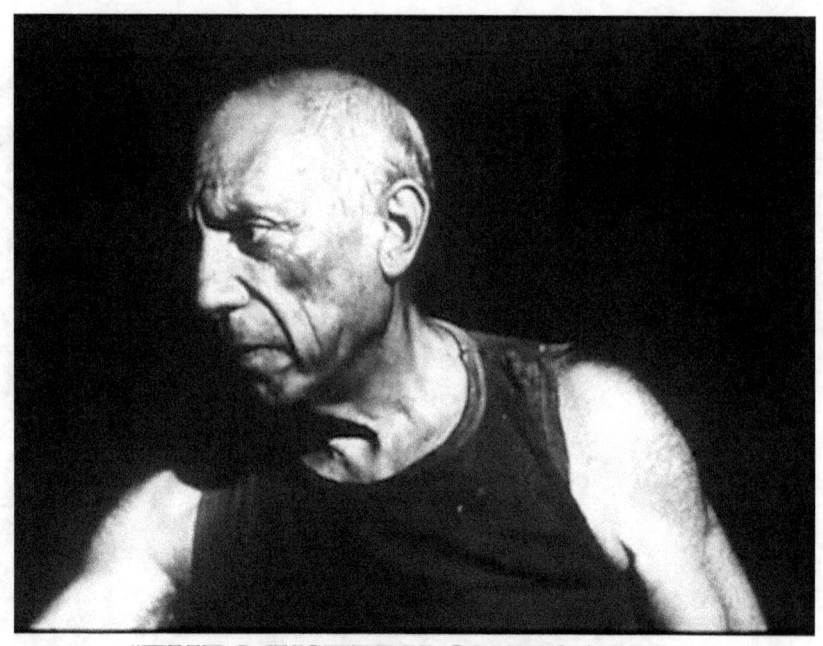

"THE MYSTERY OF PICASSO"

A Legend On Screen

"I want to go deeper," says Pablo Picasso, stopping half way through Henri-Georges Clouzot's 80 minute film on the enigmatic artist and his ability to bring ideas to life in what seems like the simplest way. Prior to this point in the film, Picasso, clad only in a pair of shorts, has been painting in a large, expansive, dark studio. The camera has been filming the reverse side of his nylon canvas, a mirrored effect which comes to life without the camera even seeing the artist, who is busy painting away on the other side. For the most part, Picasso has submitted to Clouzot's expectations, given him familiar Picasso icons and motifs, just what the public expects. This opening section, going on for quite some time, is addictive viewing, as we see strong yet very simple images come to life slowly, mostly in black (done in marker pen) and dashes of colour. However, it is clear some time in that Picasso is becoming bored with what he sees as the "superficial" work he is putting down. He suggests a change of tact, to go deeper, reveal the layers of complexity of his work. He clearly wants to expose, for this time only, the huge amount of labour and the many shades and phases one piece goes through before seeing completion. It is here, seemingly when Pablo takes control, that the film really comes to life. Taking a quick drag of a cigarette, he informs Clouzot that he is ready to go one stage further and expose the magic - and expose it he most certainly does. The final segment of the film is dazzling, showing how Picasso takes his paintings through many ideas, settings and scenarios, painting over each one to reinvent his canvas, to look at this landscape or scene from a totally different perspective. It's a rare glimpse into his genius, a by-the-numbers guide if you like to the artistic richness and variety in Picasso's art, and the bold bravery of his working methods.

The film came about when Picasso and his family made friends with Clouzot and his wife Vera in the mid 1950s. At first, Picasso must have found the idea of a film on his creative process far from interesting. Never a man to rest on his reputation or past achievements, the last thing he'd need in the studio with him was a camera crew. But when Picasso agreed to take part in the film, he insisted on a different approach. He did not consider the film serious work, but played along with Clouzot's vision, before finishing filming, going home and getting on with his real work. Maya Picasso later recalled that when Clouzot came up with the idea of drawing on nylon with a marker so it would seep through when dry, she suggested they try it out on her bra. "I only had one bra," she said, "I did not have very much. My father was not pleased." Maya's sacrifice worked and it had the desired effect. Picasso, though not considering the pieces in the film a part of his serious canon of work, was happy to join in and create some celluloid wonder.

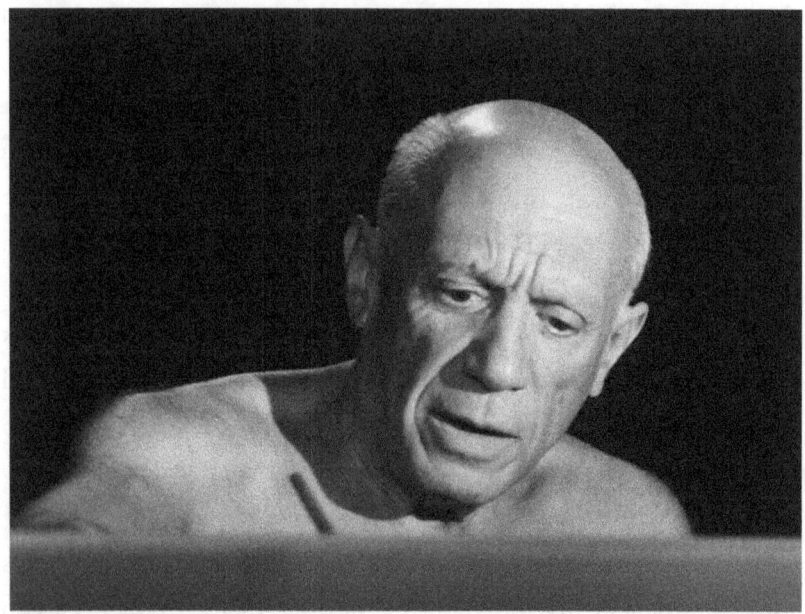

Picasso had pondered on the idea of a film capturing an art work coming to life before. In fact, he had mentioned the concept twenty years earlier in an interview with Chaiers d'Art. "It would be very interesting to record photographically, not the stages of a painting, but its metamorphoses. One would see perhaps by what course a mind finds its way towards the crystallization of its dream. But what is really very curious is to see that the picture does not change basically, that the initial vision remains almost intact in spite of appearances."

The ultimate conclusion was achieved after the film was completed, when Clouzot and Picasso destroyed all the pictures they had created for the film, meaning that they existed for this piece of documentation only. These were not, after all, pieces to be hung on a gallery, nor were they seriously considered masterpieces; they were created solely to reveal the process of their creation. Like his later paintings in the final stage of his life, this was more about showing what the artist could do when given his tools. To Clouzot it was not exactly a film about the purity of creativity, but something much more practical. "To dismantle a work of art into detached pieces," Clouzot said, "to shake these fragments about in a bag, pull them out again and fit them together like pieces of a jigsaw puzzle, can only be compared to butchery, or conjuring tricks."

The two effects the film creates when observing Picasso's creations are hugely different, and also garner varied reactions from the viewer. The first, with the ink bleeding through the reverse, highlights the childlike exuberance of Picasso's work, while the instant appearance of lines, shapes and forms ensures we see the work coming to life before our eyes in real time. It's like being in a room with Picasso, even though we cannot see him. The second part of the film has the work come to life in dissolves, with colours appearing in patches through blending, shapes, people and objects being transformed or totally covered during each merging image. The sad thing is that just as Picasso gets your interest with a certain image, a chosen colour or what seems like a definite idea in place, he sternly paints over it, sometimes coarsely, as if to erase all the work and disregard any attachment you may have had towards it during its invention. As we usually only see the finished result of a Picasso (unless its creation has been documented in photography), one is spared from the heavenly glories we might have been robbed of during the birth. Here, the glorious images are presented to us in all their splendour, before being smeared away heartlessly. It takes us inside the creation of a painting, but keeps a dream-like, fantastical atmosphere as it goes along. Though this film may uncover a bit of the mystery of the artist, it does not take away any of the magic and wonderment, the sheer joy of observing the wildly creative act, the artist let loose, feral on his canvas.

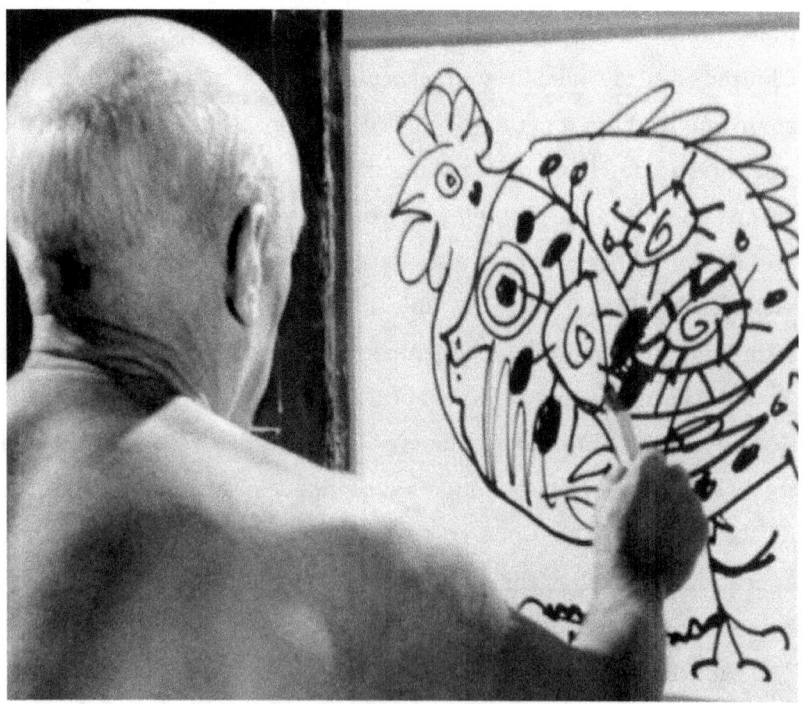

When Picasso is working, the film remains in black and white, while only his pictures, vibrant and rich, come to life with colour, thus separating the creator from his creations. And Picasso's colours,

I might add, have never looked so wonderfully full. Though the film reveals Picasso's work as it comes from his mind, down his hand and on to the page, there is little footage of the man himself, which is both a pro and con when it comes to what the film was trying to achieve and does achieve. It works in favour of keeping some mystery alive; after all, there are only a few shots of him actually holding the brush and at work before the canvas. But the fact these glimpses are so fleeting seems like a wasted opportunity from one perspective, given that there is so little footage of him at work elsewhere.

But Clouzot ensures that the shots of Picasso that are present in the finished film are unforgettable. Pablo, at the time in his mid 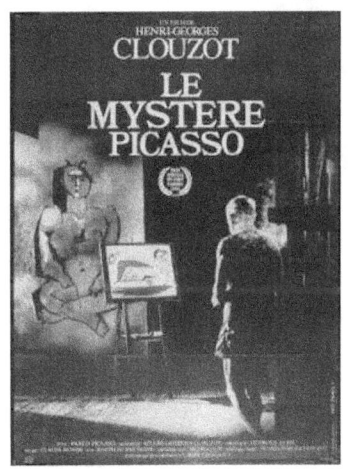 seventies, strips down to his boxer shorts due to the sheer heat of the film lights, and seems relaxed even though the director's shooting schedule clashed with his own usual paintings shifts. As we know, Picasso liked to paints solidly through the night, but here he was forced to go in bursts, stopping and starting when the film needed changing or the cameraman needed a break. Not quite capturing the real Picasso at work in his private time then, it instead gives us a cinematic, staged version of his methods. Still, Clouzot captures an intensity, especially in his eyes, even if the mood is performed somewhat. Rather than feeling like a mere painting class (albeit one with the world's finest artist), Mystery of Picasso is a performance piece snapshot, a photograph of a photograph of Picasso at work, rather than a vivid, raw document of his process.

Clouzot needs no frills or tricks when capturing Picasso, and the film relies solely on his work, and even holding back on the celebrity of Picasso himself. By keeping the artist's time on screen to a minimum, he keeps the emphasis on creativity, not the man. This, I feel, separates the film from other art movies of the time and later. Salvador Dali's Chaos and Creation, made in 1960, took a similar approach, but relied heavily on Dali the man and personality as well as focusing on the urgency of the creative act. The Mystery of Picasso though, holds itself back and is never tempted to go the easy route into Picasso clichés.

Fittingly, one man seemed to define the impact of Mystery of Picasso with a simple sentence. The man was Francois Truffaut, who wrote of the portrait: "The film is about poetry and we feel overwhelmed by it... A work by Picasso created before our very eyes! That is a miracle that, if need be, would justify the greatness of cinema."

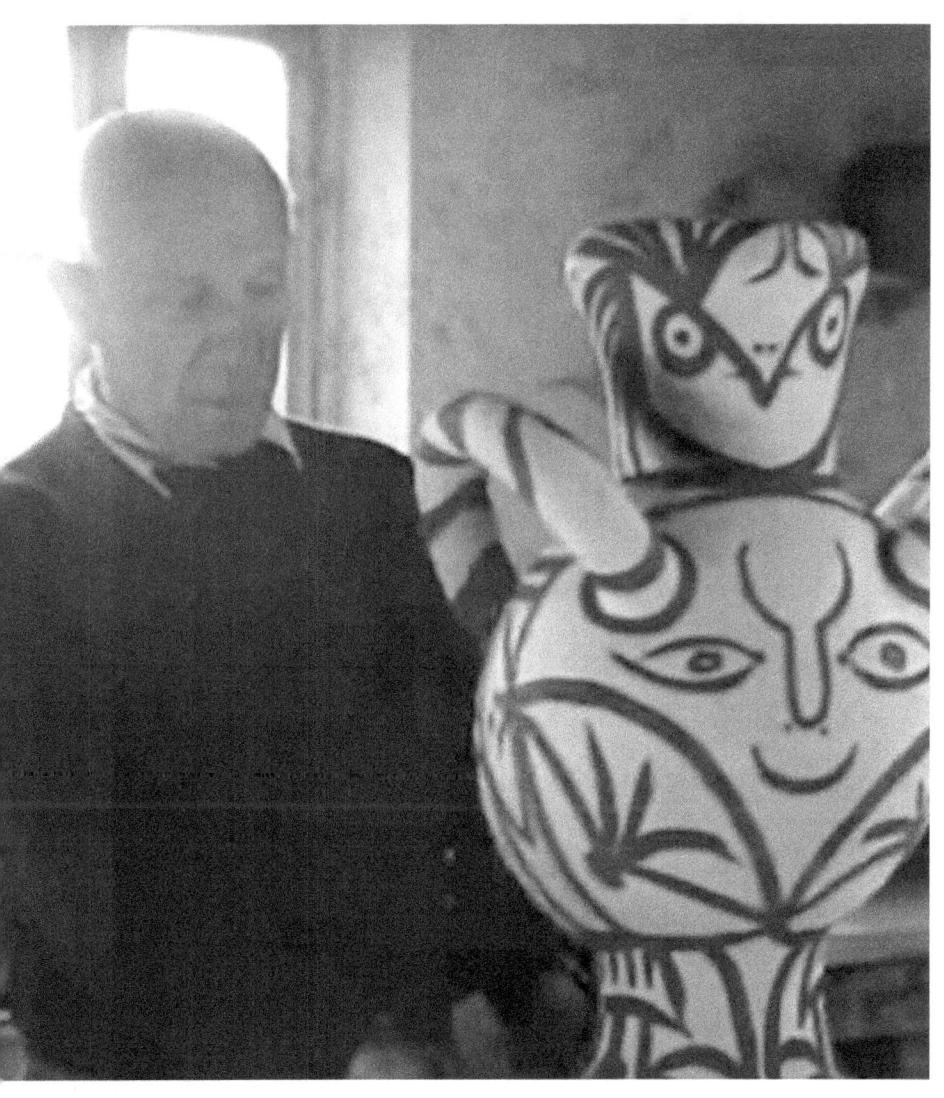

Picasso at 80.

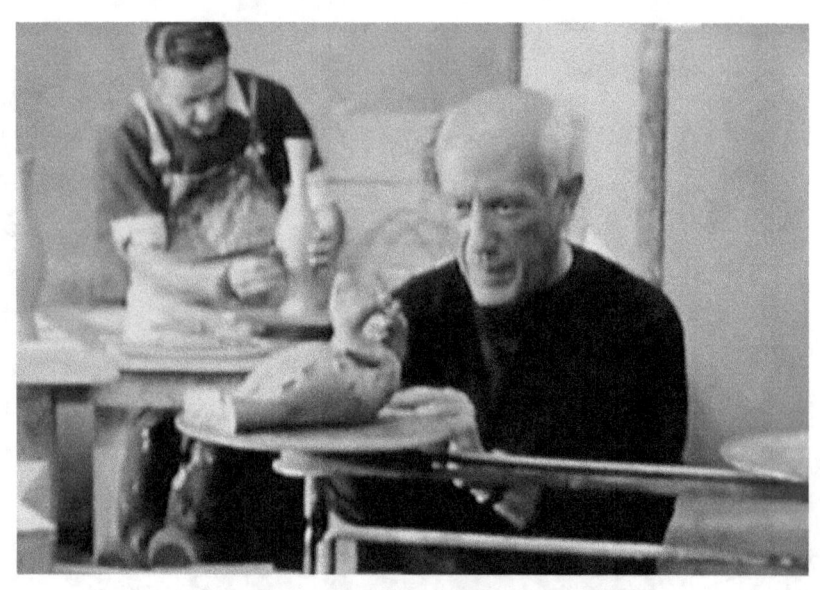

THE HEIR AFFAIR

The Case of Francoise, the Children and the

Estate of Picasso

To the public, Pablo Picasso was the joy loving millionaire artist, a beloved icon who could capture the inner soul on canvas and paper, who could channel our inner complexities with seemingly simple methods of artistic expression. He was loved, adored, worshipped, turned into a God. As his 80th birthday celebrations illustrated, where he was treated like the pope, Picasso was a modern icon. Behind the scenes though, there were other things going on which, although brushed under the carpet at the time, cannot be ignored today all these years later.

Ever since she had left almost a decade earlier, in the early to mid 1960s, Francoise was fighting for basic rights for her children, the same rights any kids should have in any standard situation involving a family split. But as Picasso had never married Francoise, and indeed had been legally wed to Olga the whole way through their ten year union, the children he had with her, Claude and Paloma, did not bear the Picasso name, meaning their entitlement to his estate and any money coming their way would be limited. She came up with all sorts of possible answers to the complexities of the situation, but none were taken seriously. In the end, Picasso's lawyer, Maitre Bacque de Sariac, came up with a strange proposal which Pablo himself had put forward. If Francoise were to divorce her current husband, Lu Simon, and legally marry Pablo, then the children could carry his name, thus automatically legitimatising and enriching their inheritance down the line. The phrase "for the sake of the children" was used time and time again, Picasso being well aware that Francoise had always looked out for their best interests. By repeating the phrase, Picasso was able to worm his way into making Francoise believe it really was the best option.

But she was having none of it, not at first anyway. She had moved on, remarried and put her life and association with Picasso into the past. But deep down Francoise knew that without the Picasso name they would not legally be entitled to as much as legitimate children. As time went on, she began to sway towards the bizarre proposal, even though she knew it was all a power trip dipping in Picasso's favour. But the truth is that things were not so good at home for Francoise. Before the children, Francoise and Luc played the perfect parents, and Luc loved being their step father. But when the kids were asleep, they fought like cats and dogs, mainly because Luc was not happy with the idea of them taking Pablo's name. To her utmost frustration, Francoise knew she would never love another man as she had Picasso, with as much passion and intensity, and this no doubt damaged her marriage to Luc; that he never really could live up to Pablo, and she, as much as she tried, could never really escape him. Still, in this case, it all came down to the kids.

As Francoise prepared to be shackled once more to the man she longed to put behind her, all for the benefit of her children, she sat down one morning and read the news. Opening the paper, she could not believe her eyes; Picasso had married Jacqueline Roque. Even as their lawyers prepared the papers and got everything in order which was needed for Francoise's legal marriage to him, Picasso had quickly dashed off and married Jacqueline. By the time it was public news, the same time Francoise found out about it, Picasso had been married for twelve days. It was 1961, and Picasso was almost eighty. Yet here he was, married once again to a woman decades his junior, still toying with the life of his former lover, Francoise. Though she was annoyed, at least, thought Francoise, Paloma and Claude had now been legally granted the Picasso name.

Relationships began to sour here after on all fronts, and Jacqueline was not so fond of seeing Clause and Paloma; perhaps because they reminded her of Francoise, her famous predecessor. When Francoise published her memoir damning Picasso, he had the children banned from his home. Though this act was to hurt Francoise, it also hurt the children, and ultimately himself too, though he would not have known this at the time; or, more to the point, dared to admit it. Sadly, he never saw them again. From now on, it was him, Jacqueline and the few chosen few, a very small, trusted amount of people who Picasso felt were worthy of inclusion in his world. Work became more intense here after, more self critical, self probing and stark. He poured on the colours, but beneath the surface was a blackness that had not been present in his earlier paintings.

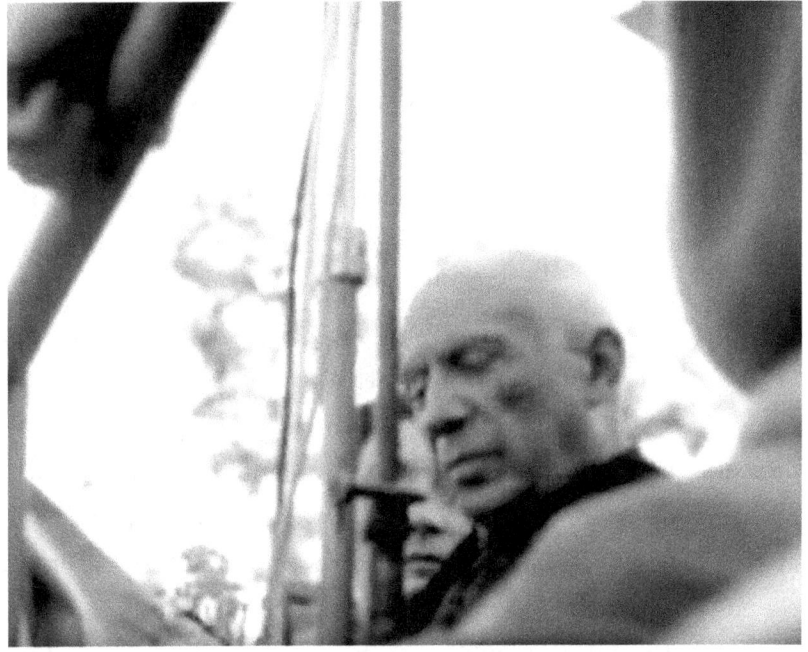

Picasso during lavish public celebrations for his 80th birthday.

Looking back in the 1990s, Claude was blunt with his assessment of the situation involving his father. "Yes, everybody's been retelling the story so many hundreds of times, and not very accurately or very sensibly, so I think a good part of my private life doesn't belong to me any more. In a way, it doesn't interest me any longer, except that I know, and I can assert the difference between certain fantastic stories and things closer to reality. I retain a few personal feelings, more intimate memories, which I don't even like to share because, by

93

sharing, I'm robbed of them. There is very little left that is not a historical fact. Most of it now for me is art history; it's not even my own life."

That said, Claude also had fond memories of his father from the days when Pablo and Francoise were together, saying he never got annoyed with them and preferred the company of children to adults. "My father always said that when children or animals are in the studio there is nothing to worry about, but when adults walk into the studio it's a catastrophe. Because they always will step on something, knock things over..."

Still, the conclusion to the story is a sad one. Early photographs of Picasso with Claude show a man head over heels in love with his young boy, worshipping his youth and energy. It's rather tragic to think that in the next two decades, Picasso would have him banished from his home. As Picasso turned 80, the world celebrated the ongoing life of the world's greatest artist. Picasso on the other hand closed himself off and shut out the world, installing high powered security gates and thus building a literal and symbolic wall against everyone on the outside he no longer trusted.

"At the end," Picasso said, "nobody can see anything except himself. Thanks to the never ending search for reality. He ends in black obscurity."

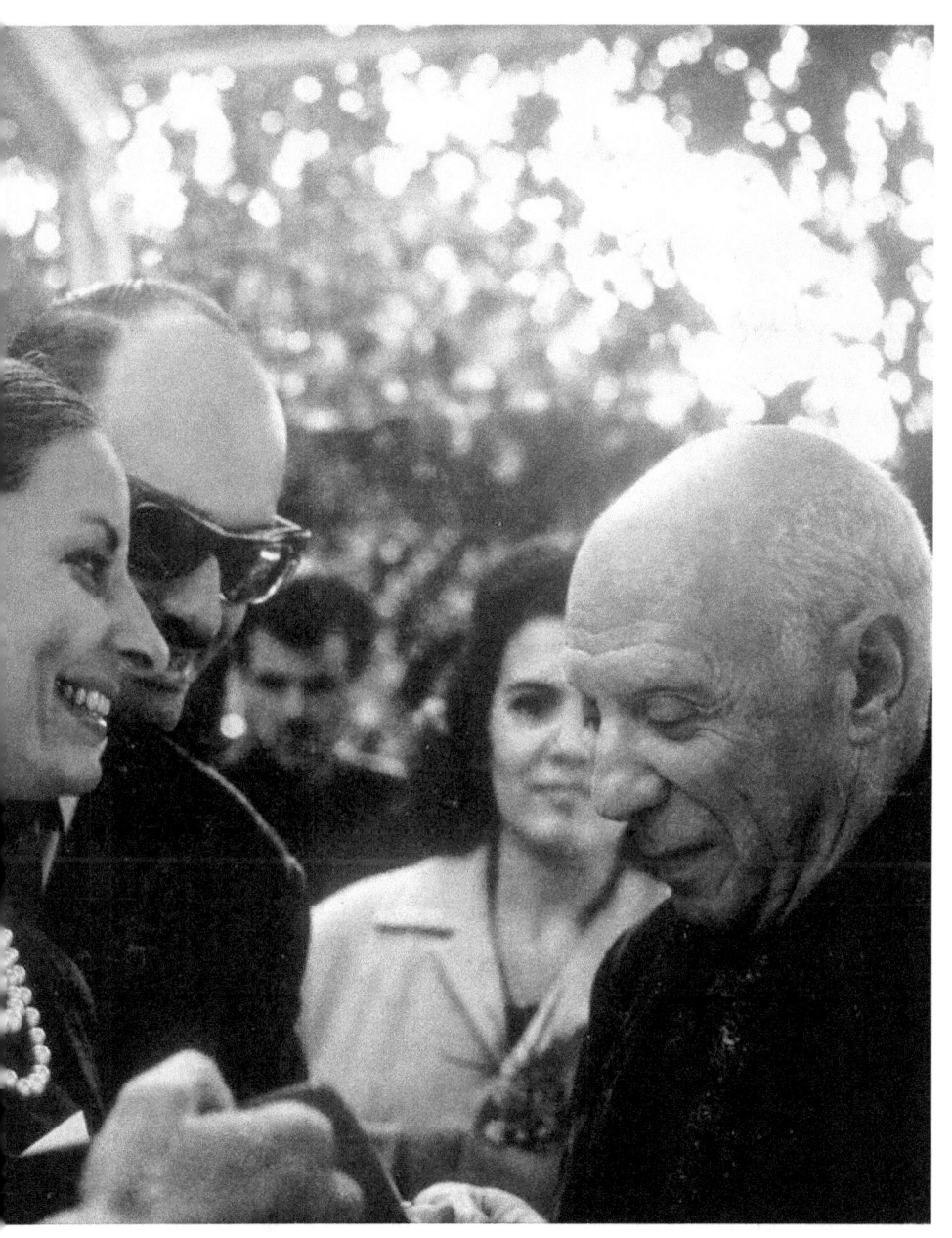

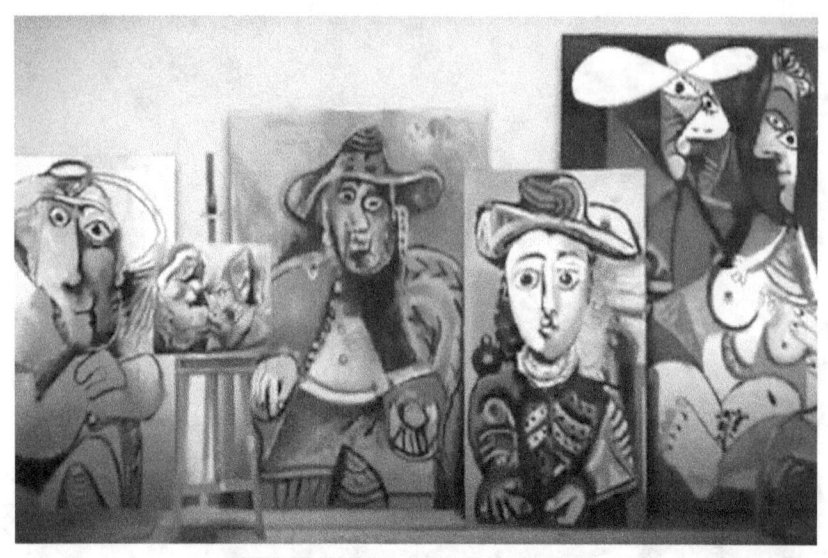

THE FINAL BURST

The Aging Icon in the Age of Reinvention

As he shifted into the sixties, approaching the age of 80, Picasso found himself in a curious position. He was no longer at the forefront of the modern art scene, and was hardly seen as a vital creative force in its change and development. However, he was still a God to most modern artists, and as such his work and reputation elevated him above the rest almost automatically, even as Pop Art took over the scene and Picasso's more direct influence seemed to dim. But he enjoyed the status of an innovator, a living legend, even if he was no longer a part of the mainstream and his sole position on the pedestal was a lonely one. Now, he was becoming increasingly more personal, turning the mirror around to himself, and no longer reflecting the world outside at all. He would reinvent the old classics once again, although perhaps in more drastic forms, and strange perversions began to seep in as the sixties became the seventies. But he enjoyed a healthy creative decade, even if his work highlights the fact he was in a constant race against time, battling the inevitability of death.

He began the decade with a hugely successful exhibition at the Tate in London. The UK had not been as open to Picasso as the rest of the world, but there was a dramatic shift when 270 of his works were unveiled at the prestigious venue. Picassomania was in full

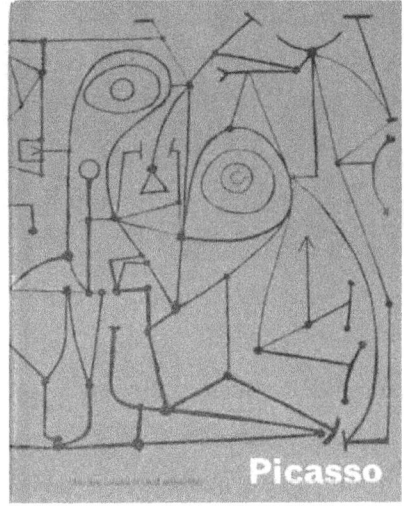

swing. Before this, the rigid traditions of the British Isles had resisted the urge of taking Picasso seriously. Modern art was that most awful of things - modern. Winston Churchill even made jokes about kicking Pablo in the "something something", and Evelyn Waugh famously signed off his letters with "Death to Picasso". But all this changed with the Tate retrospective, which elevated Picasso to the status he enjoyed in the rest of the world.

By 1961, he had finally married Jacqueline, and they moved together into their new home, Notre Dame de Vie. Though this rather lavish home, like La Californie before it, did not look like the dwelling of a Communist party member, Picasso did not live luxuriously within its walls, sticking to a simplistic life and remaining a good party member. He was 80 now, another landmark age, which meant that though he was happy to be alive, Picasso felt the presence of death even closer to him.

97

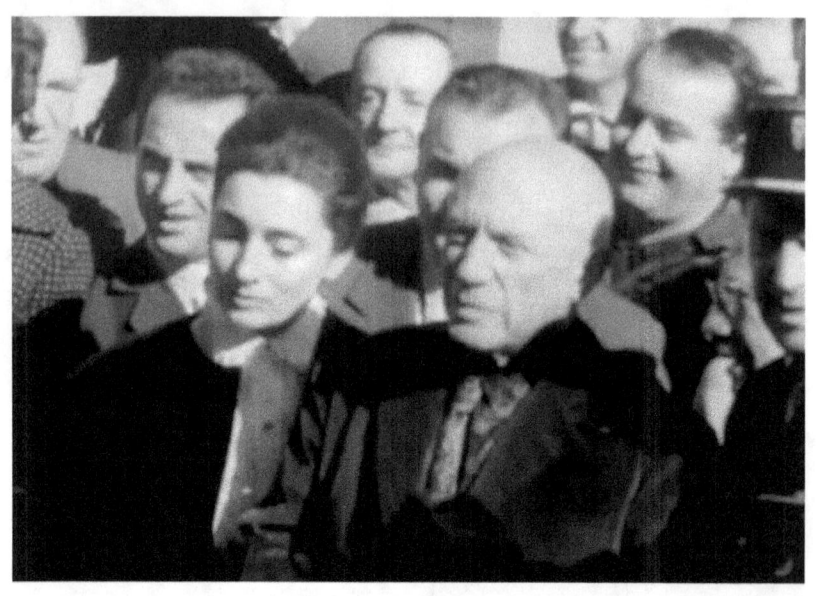

Picasso and Jacqueline in the early sixties.

In 1962, he painted over 70 portraits of Jacqueline, his muse and inspiration throughout the final stages. Picasso's friend and biographer John Richardson is more than qualified to assess Jacqueline's place in the Picasso story, and compared her, in an interview with Arts Desk, with other Picasso muses.

"Jacqueline was a whole different thing," he said. "I loved Dora Maar but she was very difficult to get close to because she had this piety which she wore like armour and you had to watch your words with her. You said the wrong thing, she would get terribly angry, whereas Jacqueline was this girl from nowhere. I just felt she was the only person for him. She was consumed with love for him and would do anything for him. He told this story about his sister Conchita, when he swore that he would never ever paint again if her life was spared, and he did paint and she died, and this he only told to the women in his life, for some reason, I suppose as a sort of warning. And she clearly must have very early on felt that she was ready for it. Like all martyrs, she was blind to so much, blind to the damage he was doing to other members of the Picasso family."

The fact that Jacqueline was "up for the challenge" so to speak explains why she could be anything, everything and nothing to Picasso whenever and however he felt. She would always be there (literally always) and do whatever he asked. The fact she was not an egg that needed to be cracked like Dora and Francoise worked in both their favours; Jacqueline had an easier go with him by being the obedient wife and standing by him no matter what, and Picasso, getting older and less likely to have the energy for a "fight", found her easier, less a challenge and just the kind of support he needed at that time. That said, she also inspired positivity in his work, a good thing in an artist's later years.

As more acclaim came his way, such as the opening of the Museu Picasso in Barcelona, Pablo was surprised when he came under a sudden attack. Picasso was devastated when his former ally, John Berger, wrote a damning book on what he saw as his failures as an artist, the loss of direction he had apparently suffered in recent times. Berger accused Picasso of sexism, only being concerned with what happened to men, and relying too much on his own personality, now well known to the public, rather than pushing his art into new areas as he once had with cubism, surrealism and political works like Guernica. Though Berger was a fan of Picasso's war themed work of the 1930s, he was critical of his wealth, the fact he had not suffered through the war like others had. "Just after the Second World War

Picasso bought a house in the South of France and paid for it with one still-life," Berger writes in his book, The Success and Failure of Picasso. "Picasso has now in fact transcended the need for money. Whatever he wishes to own, he can acquire by drawing it. The truth has become a little like the fable of Midas."

Berger may have had some valid points, but he was arguably misguided on most accounts. Either way, the harsh criticism hurt Picasso, and by now, he was appearing more mortal than ever before. In 1965 he collapsed and was taken, in complete secrecy, to a hospital in Paris. He was starting to appear frailer, now surpassing the age of 84, and being unable to hide the fact. It was later revealed he had been suffering from a stomach ulcer, though heaven forbid anyone should know about it. He and Jacqueline kept it under wraps, even though Picasso gave clues away by asking friends who had had stomach ulcers what they had done to alleviate the pain. The mask he wore for the press and public, that he was the immortal artist, invulnerable and made of stone, was starting to slip.

Still, the press learned of his ill health, and dissected his state. After an operation, Picasso spent a month in recuperation at the hospital before he returned home to his country home. He hired extra security, locked the gates and closed the curtains. No one - and that truly meant no one - was going to invade his fortress now. Jacqueline took over as his carer, and exhausted herself through this era, going to the bank, getting the food shopping in and performing all the physically demanding tasks the ageing artist could no longer do. There had been a shift. When they had first met, Picasso was in his early seventies, though in his spirit seemed much younger. Now, he was undeniably an old man in every way.

100

Sadly, the operation meant that Picasso was no longer able to stand up comfortably when painting, so now had to be seated when creating art. Though his depression deepened in this era, he learned to enjoy etching, which he excelled in during the latter part of the 1960s. Picasso's friend Angela Rosengart later recalled Jacqueline saying "Great, life has started again." Now that Picasso was back at work, in her mind it meant all was well. She was denying his age and decreasing health, but was happy to put on a brave face and convince herself that Picasso was as vital and vibrant as ever.

In 1969, Picasso was shaken by the sudden death of his long time friend Jaime Sabartes. It reminded him of his own mortality, as if he needed more reminding given his recent health issues. Sabartes had been a loyal friend since the days of his youth, a man Picasso enjoyed paying pranks on and ribbing mercilessly. He knew Sabartes worshipped him, and used this to his advantage. When he passed away, a little piece of Pablo went with him. As old friends died, allies left his side, and family members drifted away, the Picasso circle grew smaller. By the late 1960s, he was accepting of his legacy but uninterested in courting those who showered him with acclaim. He did, however, make his last donation to the Museu Picasso in 1969, giving 900 works from his own private collection. Still, you wouldn't catch him roaming the halls as Dali would his own self made museum in the 1980s; Picasso was too busy in his own world, painting, working, toiling away to forget the worries of his life, and to block them out with paint, shapes and forms.

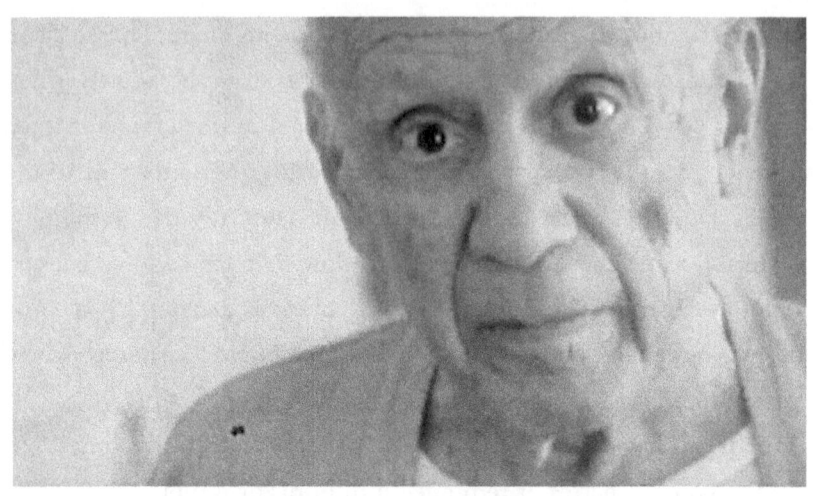

"The old man couldn't seem to get his mind off sex."

- Calvin Thomas, the New Yorker

The final Picasso works came in explosive bursts. Though often sidelined as the obscene scribblings of a dirty old man, there is an energy in the work he did from 1968 to 1971. It is less about the beauty (or lack thereof) of the finished work, but more about the process, the thrill and satisfaction of getting the canvas filled, revealing the fundamental tools and methods available to the artist. He had always felt the compulsion to paint, ever since his boy hood in fact when he promised to give it up if the Lord spared his young sister (he didn't incidentally, resulting in a life long addiction to painting); but as he approached 90, he felt that working at such a rate would prolong his life. Indeed, as he splashed his canvas with wild brushstrokes, Picasso felt youthful and alive, even if the body of his, still strong for an old man, was weakening by the day. Each new blank canvas promised something fresh and beautiful, and the hastiness of some of this work shows that Picasso was not concerned with capturing perfection, but an essence of his urgency. There is a fevered delirium here, the impression that Picasso was not thinking too much about what he was doing, but exorcising his own demons, thinking only of himself, certainly not the viewer, the observer or the future. Did Picasso care how these pieces were going to be viewed? No, of course not, but there was nothing new there. Pablo was merely following his true inner voice, the one that had guided him since the late 1800s when he began this journey. Now he was nearing its end, but for him that was no reason to stop and quit. He had to soldier on, prove that he was alive and a valid voice after all these years.

"Art experts and critics are divided about the artistic merit of the late works," wrote Art News in 2007, as the later years began to gain some admiration on a larger scale. "But prices keep rising, along with the broader art market, as the availability of earlier Picassos narrows. The jump in prices is particularly remarkable because the supply of late Picassos is plentiful, report several auction house experts. Though Picasso was always prolific, the sheer magnitude of his output in later years - hundreds of paintings and drawings - is interpreted by many experts as a sign of the artist's attempt to stave off death. The artist's late works continue to be far less costly than major ones from his Blue, Rose and Cubist periods. His 1905 Boy with a Pipe reached $104.2 million (ANL, 5/25/04) at Sotheby's in 2004 and still holds the record for the most expensive painting sold at public auction. However, several experts point out, the late works are increasingly viewed as innovative, expressive, uninhibited and radical."

While Picasso's earlier, more iconic work has become the modern classical art of our time, the later work produced in the era of Pop Art, the age of controversial reinvention, fits with ease alongside the current trend setting work of the day. No doubt, these works impressed Andy Warhol in their speediness, and key 80s figures like Julian Schnabel and Jean-Michel Basquait must surely have been inspired by the themes, especially Picasso's knack of reinventing classic art and making it his own. The later works then, seem to be fitting with their time frame and the art eras to come in the following generations, though remain on the side lines of fashion.

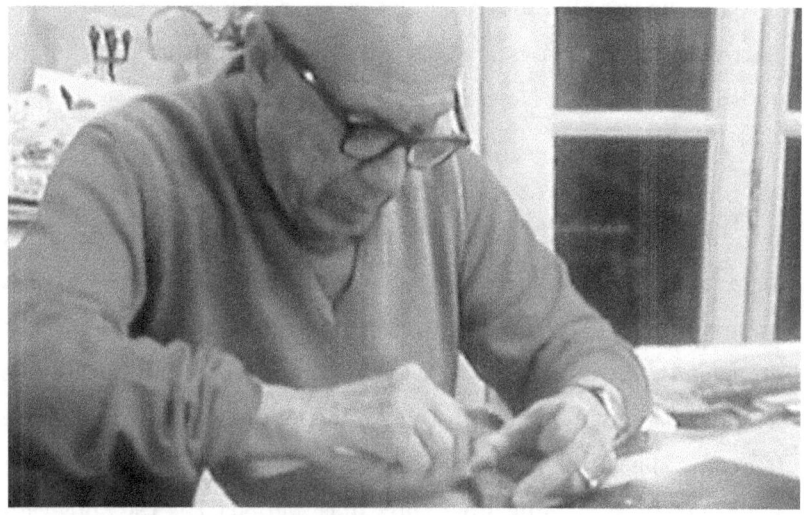

Still working, still searching for a truth.

John Richardson, an obsessive devotee of Picasso, has been honest with his criticism of some of Picasso's fifties and sixties work; in particular what he saw the tired politics of War and Peace and Massacre in Korea, the obviousness which was certainly not there in

Guernica and his war themed work from the Second World War. Richardson though, has been kind about the work Picasso put out in the late sixties and early seventies; if not aesthetically, then conceptually at least. He feels the work exposes an inner strength and defiance which is inspiring, laudable even.

Though many collectors initially found the final work garish, crass and crude, and Richardson admitted he was merely "tossing them off", he concluded that the work was "a wonderful field for people, many of whom have very little experience of art but want something bigger and splashier in colour." Indeed, anyone baffled by Picasso's cubism, depressed by the sombre Blue Period or baffled by the deconstructive force of some of his most well known images may find something to grasp and hold dear in the last paintings and drawings. They are terribly moving works, though only in their mood and heaviness, not particularly in their aesthetic qualities. One cannot compress the feeling one gets of desperation, a lust for a youth long gone, a clinging to the joys of existence and a shackled pain to the agony of reality. They are his most human and flawed works, and Picasso seems scared, frightened even, for the first time in his artistic life.

"He was very tired and very old," art dealer Jan Krugier later said of this period, "and not everything he made was okay. He might make one painting every day - and out of every ten, maybe two were okay and the other eight were not, and Picasso himself did not really care about the difference." Clearly, it was no longer about the finished result, but the process, the act itself. Picasso always said a creative act is firstly a destructive one, and here he risked destroying his own myth and reputation with works that for the most part went straight over people's heads.

Picasso was no longer living a public life, and though still a celebrity in the fullest sense of the word (art's first true star no less) his life was that of a hermit, living on his own cloud. Jacqueline had become his protector, the keeper of his gate, and no one she thought would distract him was allowed inside. Picasso was cut off, choosing to work, work, work as people his age were giving into death. Clearly, he lived out his final years, months and days doing exactly what he wanted to do - creating, painting, drawing, tearing through countless canvases and note pads in a bid to fend off the reaper.

"Quite free from the sovereign thrift and the flawless overall control of earlier Picasso, the work went its own way," the New York Times wrote of later Picasso in 1984, just as the paintings were growing in importance. "It had its own weight, its own momentum and its own ambitions. It had a variety that was quite simply prodigious. There were people who, for one reason or another, found it inconvenient; but eventually, in the 1980's, it has turned out to have an enormous influence upon young painters the world over. For the first time in many years, the impact of Picasso upon those trying to find themselves in paint has been liberating, rather than repressive. The headlong brushwork, the tumultuous narrative element, the readiness to take any and every risk that came along, the contempt for taboos of no matter what kind - all have become precious to a new generation of painters... Whereas the masterpieces of his earlier years have come to seem both remote and daunting, late Picasso has, for the generation that came of age around 1975, a direct and heady appeal. It is as if he had stepped out of the day before yesterday and become part of today. In painting, late Picasso means images that are meaty, forthright, high and free in colour and quite often slapdash in appearance. Where once he had done as he liked with painting, it now seemed as if painting were doing as it liked with him."

Though they might be a morbid pleasure to look at, these later works are also heavy, suffocating and claustrophobic in their joint defiance and acceptance of Picasso's various fears. To look is one thing, but to think, comprehend and understand these works, at least on the levels it is possible to do so, reveals a man in the harsh, bleak winter of decay. Dripping from these paintings quite often is an unquenchable desire, a dark sexual obsession, and perhaps the cruellest reality of all for Picasso, the final dread of impotency. For a man driven by carnal delights, the lack of sexual activity in his final age must surely have been crushing. Still, rather than sit and cry about his inability to love, Picasso put it down on canvas, often to breathtaking results. The Kiss, which he painted in 1969, is possibly the saddest, most moving and most beautiful painting of his final five or so years. In the grey and blue punctuated work, Picasso is kissing Jacqueline, but it is not a meeting of the lips born out of desire, but duty, marital loyalty and friendship. There is no desire here and neither party seems to be enjoying the kiss very much. The old man, clearly Picasso in disguise, is bald, scraggy, bearded and his best days are behind him. He tries to be an object of desire at this late stage, and clearly longs for her flesh. But the eroticism is not there, and his role seems fatherly. Jacqueline, though not aroused or alive with desire for the man, seems protected, warm, loved and content. Picasso's role has shifted from woman eating Minotaur to paternal guide and keeper. Still, he is tormented by the truth of this transition, desperate to be the lover once again. Perhaps Picasso had always taken his ability to make love for granted, thinking he would always be able to do so. Now that he saw death before him, he had to accept the time he did have left would be without sexual desire and erotic passion.

For some though, it isn't just about the work itself, but how it was presented and hung, and the environment it finds itself in. When the Tate Gallery exhibited his later works in 1988, London Review of Books wrote of the importance of organisation and atmosphere. "At the Tate Picasso's late paintings seem almost to be different paintings from those they seemed to be at Beaubourg. There they looked, by common consent, more aggressive and explosive and electric, here more luminous, more beautiful, more grand. The differences in the selection, the hang and the ground-plan have not been crucial enough to account for so extreme a difference of effect. Clearly the Tate's having daylight, a light that is soft and diffuse, must be relevant, but the difference has also been there, though not as extreme, at times when the lighting has been mixed or purely electric. In Paris the spaces were not enclosed by the walls: above the tops of the manifestly temporary partitions you could see those hyperactive Beaubourg ceilings. Here, the moveable walls reach the ceilings and these are vaulted, so that the paintings are surmounted by an amplitude of space in which to breathe. Those vaulted spaces do not suit every sort of art, and there are some paintings in the show which look less telling than they did in Paris. But others look greater than I have seen them look before... And by and large the paintings do look very much at home in these vaulted spaces."

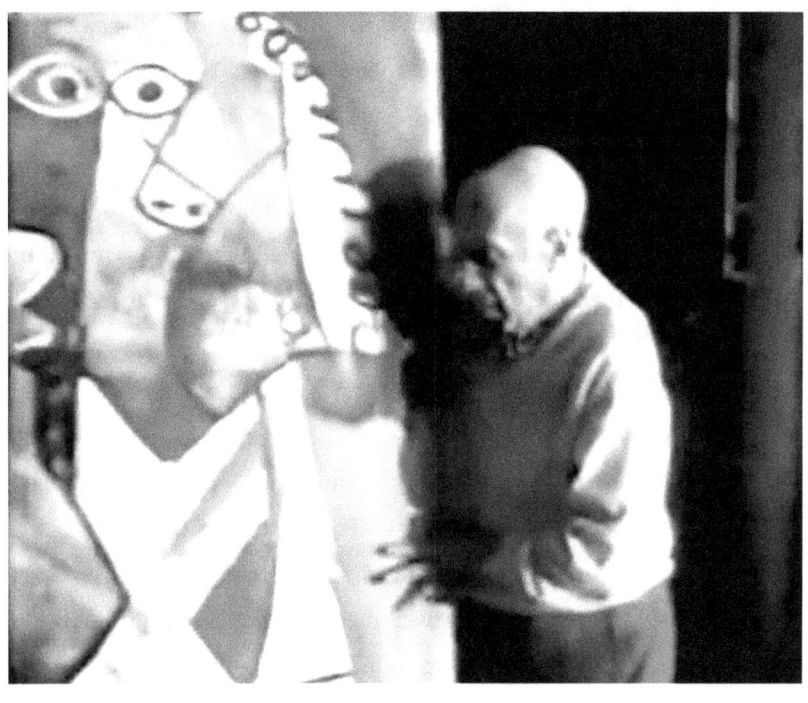

Putting their true aesthetic merits aside (after all, beauty is in the eye of the beholder, and this is no more true than with art) there is an excitement in these pictures which goes way beyond their limited lives on the canvas. They have entered another zone altogether, the mythical area given over to the artist's best work. And it isn't necessarily there because of its visual quality, but for its bravery, its sense of daring, its boldness. Picasso was splashing the paint like a man possessed, and nothing could stop him. The fact the world on the outside was honouring him left right and centre, unveiling huge exhibitions dedicated to his legacy, seemed not to matter one jot. For Picasso, life was now work. He would paint all day until the wee hours of the night; creating, toying, grasping for something; a secret, a key to eternal life. Through his art he had already gained a kind of immortality at this point, and he must have surely known his finest work was going to be looked at and admired for decades, if not centuries to come. These days that is a given, but it is hard to imagine Picasso was really thinking this when he did his last works, his childish musketeer pictures, his endless self portraits, his obsessive sexual work. Picasso surely did not ponder on where this work would sit in the full retrospective view of his career, and if he had been thinking that he would not have been the true artist he so stubbornly remained. These paintings were not genius, they were not technically great and they certainly weren't visually pleasing; but they were real, raw, and often disturbing. At times they remain hard to look at; though, in line with man's perversions, they are also impossible to look away from. The work led up to the final act of a play that took in drama, comedy, power and, ultimately, tragedy.

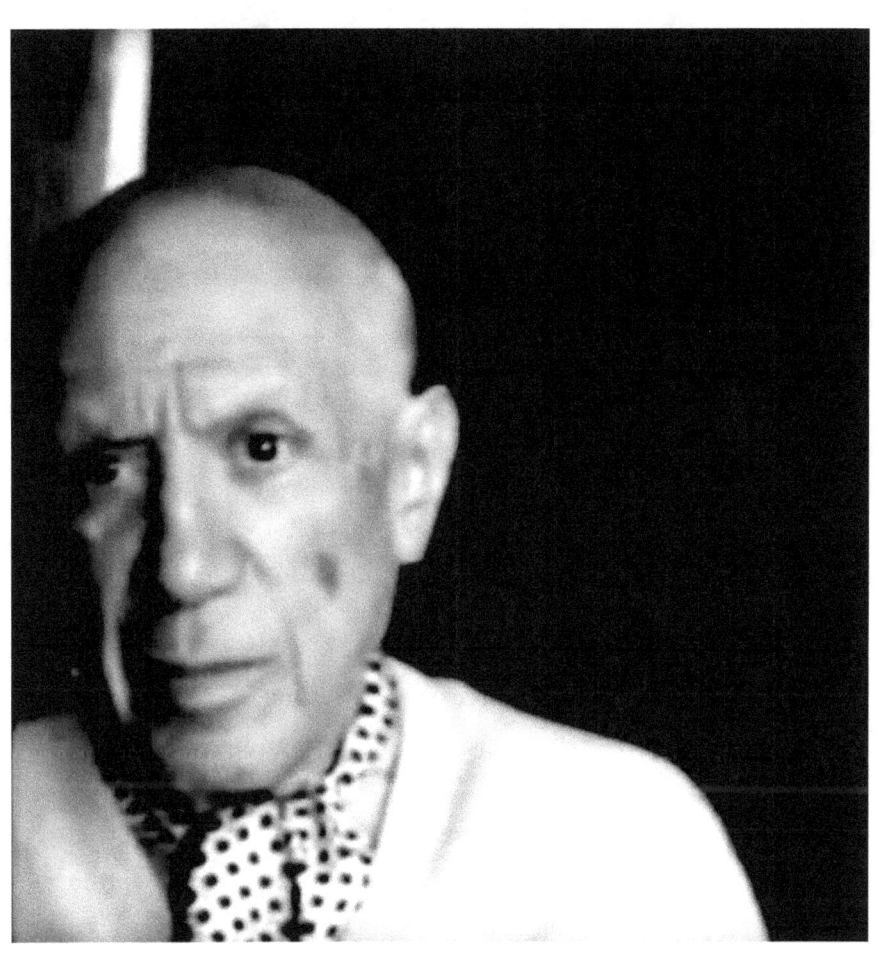

Picasso near the end...

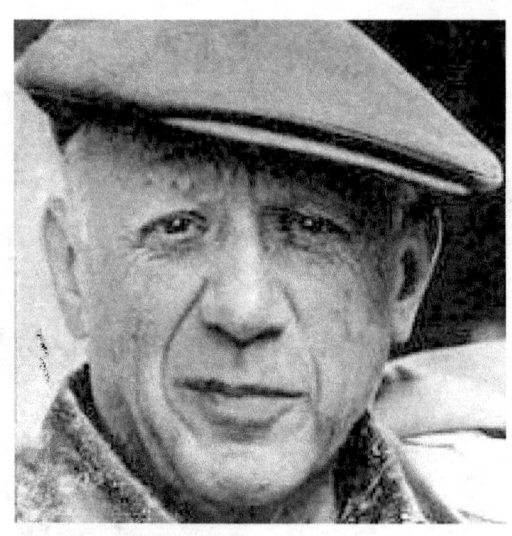

THE DEATH OF PICASSO

And in the End...

"When I die, it will be a shipwreck, and as when a huge ship sinks, many people all around will be sucked down with it." - Picasso

On the 30th of June in 1972, Picasso drew his final self portrait, aptly titled Self Portrait Facing Death. If Picasso felt the reaper drawing nearer, the picture genuinely reflected that. Rather than musing on the idea or image of death as an abstract certainty, a philosophical concept and all it entails, Pablo was staring it straight on, considering it as a literal reality coming his way sooner rather than later. His friend Pierre Daix paid Pablo a visit and saw the newly completed work. "Picasso held the drawing beside his face to show that the expression of fear was a contrivance." When he paid the artist another visit three months later, he saw that Picasso had deepened the lines on the drawing. "He did not blink. I had the sudden impression that he was staring his own death in the face, like a good Spaniard. This was not simple courage, but the courage of his conviction. With the correspondence between his work and his daily life, it was to be expected that the anticipation of his death would assume its place."

Given Picasso once said "I am Spanish, I like sadness," he was clearly inspired by the very idea of his demise, but chilled to the bone by its inevitability. This muddled feeling is there in the work, the duality of fear and inspiration, the paradoxical pairing of dread and fascination. This had been a journey through life; a journey lived through art and documented by it every step of the way. With Picasso centre stage in this colourful saga, it was now at its end, though the vibrant fiction had transformed into a grotesque, stark truth. Picasso had been "close to death" for two decades now, though by the middle of 1972, he could almost certainly smell it lingering behind him, breathing its cold air down the back of his neck.

At this stage, Picasso has totally shut the world out, with only a tiny selection of trusted people allowed anywhere near his fortress. Jacqueline gets much of the blame for this, but it may have been down to Picasso's insistence too that no one be let through the gates. After all, he told his close friend and documenter, Helene Parmelin, "You live a poet's life, and I a convict's." It was most certainly self inflicted, and the artist inevitably chooses to live their life in a closed off bubble. But Picasso could perhaps grasp the tragedy of his existence, and see himself filling the role of the man hiding the keys to his own jail cell.

To get an idea of how Picasso felt in his final years, one must compare the work he did to that of the other great artists. Salvador Dali, too ill and infirm to paint at all in his final decade or so, was holed up in his own man-made museum, fading away as each month passed by; bed ridden, unable to sleep, haunted by life, a shadow of his former self. Claude Monet, knowing the end was near, painted Water Lilies, comforted by their beauty; while Van Gogh, tormented in his own way, turned to the Sunflower for inspiration. Most telling of all is how Picasso's biggest contemporary, Henri Matisse, filled out his final days as a bed ridden artist, experimenting like a child with the art of cut outs. He was unable to paint, being too ill to concentrate on the art for too long, so he picked up a pair of scissors and began to toy with the medium that was new to him. Fittingly, when he died, Picasso was heard to say, "At the end of the day, there is only Matisse." For his part, Picasso did not distract himself from the impending cloud of death, but stared it in the face, challenged it almost, like the matador to the bull, to see if it really did have the nerve to take him away. In the final years, Picasso had created more work than any other time, clinging on to life by keeping his artistic drive alive, and creating an illusion of youth, the idea that it was impossible for him to die when he was creating so much work. Never resting on his past laurels, Picasso looked on ahead, making sure he viewed each new work as an equal to his legendary masterpieces. If he stopped for a second, he was surely to die.

But the final self portrait is a bleak admittance, though still not a submission, that all is clearly not well. Just like he had painted the cow's skull after the death of Julio Gonzalez, Picasso used his own head, his own skull, to predict his own fall. His eyes in the picture are the first thing you are drawn to as a spectator, the fact they are so big, so afraid, terrified even, by the finality that awaits him. But he also looks brave, defiant, not ready to go in spirit, even if his body might be willing to give in.

By the various accounts of the last year or so building towards Picasso's death, even the least sympathetic ones, it was most certainly a strange time. In August of 1972, his grandson Pablito arrived at Picasso's home on a motorcycle to see his famous Granddad. Not only was he turned away, but when he would not leave he found himself besieged by dogs, and his motorbike was tossed into a ditch. Evidently, if you weren't on the guest list, Picasso was going to make that very clear to you.

At the end of 1972, Picasso was admitted into hospital with pulmonary congestion. No further details were given, and Jacqueline assured their closest allies that everything was OK. Edouard Pignon recalled a rather sad telephone conversation from a tired out Picasso begging him to come around to see in the New Year with him. "Just come!" he said, nearly begging. How could he refuse such a request? During Picasso's final New Year's Eve party, his friends found themselves around Picasso's bed, and Jacqueline, clearly in denial that her husband was close to death, did not seem to see the sadness of such a gathering. Pignon over heard Picasso urging Jacqueline to make sure no one passed on the rumours that he was ill. But he *was* ill, and as much as he tried to cover it up, he could not deny the truth, not from his friends, nor himself, nor Jacqueline. But keeping up the illusion, perhaps mostly for the ever reliant Jacqueline, Picasso got dressed and came downstairs to entertain his friends at the New Year shindig. Almost as if nothing was wrong, Picasso was the old Picasso once again, if only for one more night.

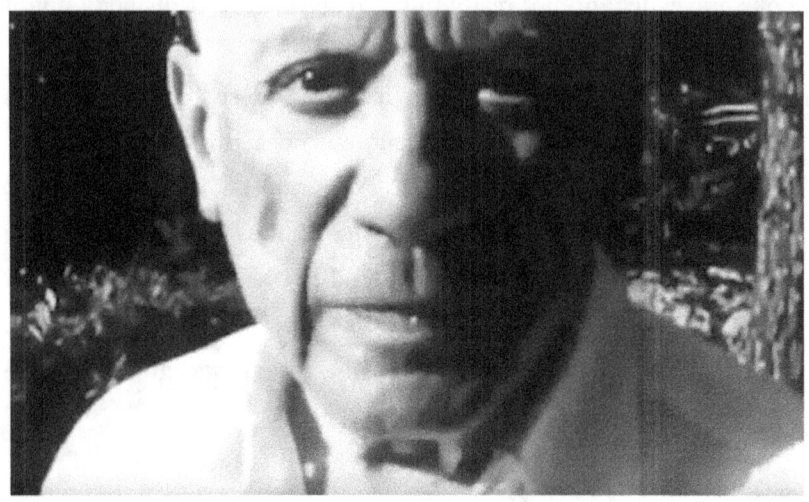

Picasso looking more intense than ever, nearing the end of his life.

As the next four months went on, Picasso weakened, and he found it increasingly difficult to not face up to the truth, even if Jacqueline convinced herself everything was OK. In April, he wrote to Marie-Therese and told her, rather curiously, that she was the only woman he had ever loved. Did he mean it, or was it a last minute attempt to manipulate the woman who had never really gotten over Picasso? No one will ever truly know, but it seems an odd admittance that Picasso did not love Jacqueline or Francoise, and slightly hard to swallow.

Three days before his death, Picasso was on the phone to Edouard Pignon, speaking about his friend's upcoming exhibition. He was in good spirits, telling Pignon to make sure he put in "mountains of breasts and bottoms". Pablo played it well that day, trying to convince everyone he was still the mischievous old devil. Jacqueline too could not help but interject; she came on the line and insisted to Pignon, "You see, everything is fine!"

Of course, she was lying to herself. Picasso was not fine. On the 8th of April at the break of dawn after working until 3 a.m., Jacqueline was forced to call Picasso's Paris based cardiologist, Pierre Bernal, though she did not openly articulate that it was not a visit she was after, but help, and fast! He boarded a plane and headed out to Picasso's villa in Mougins. When he arrived, the local doctor was already by Picasso's side, where he was gasping for breath. Jacqueline was in a state of panic, pacing and repeating that everything would be OK. She left the room eventually, unable to accept that Picasso was dying. Bernal could see he was at the end now, even if Picasso was not sure of the fact himself.

Picasso called out for Jacqueline from the bedroom, like a child calling for his mother, while Jacqueline's daughter Catherine sat with the doctor, who told her it was not going well. She could see that much for herself of course, even if her mother could not. When Picasso tried to talk it came out like a cry of despair, and before long his heart and lungs started to give up. "You are wrong not to be married," he told the doctor, "it is useful." These were reportedly the last audible words before Picasso's voice became nothing more than a sad muffle. At quarter to 12, Bernal gave Picasso a booster and realised his heart had stopped. He attempted to bring him back with a cardiac massage, but nothing happened. Finally, it was the end. He closed Picasso's eyes, yet Jacqueline denied he was gone. When someone coughed in the room, Jacqueline became excited that it was Picasso. His pulse was checked once again. Picasso was dead.

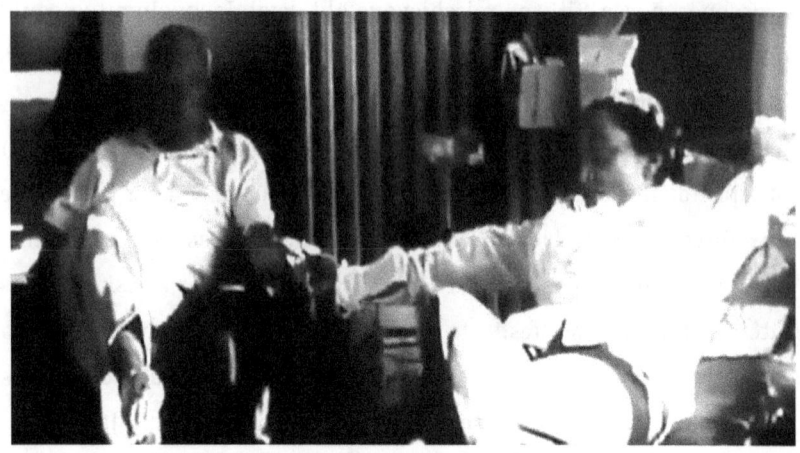

Pablo and Jacqueline, inseparable to the end.

The obituaries came flooding in, for the world's most famous artist was no longer among us. "The artist Pablo Picasso has died of a heart attack at his chateau near Cannes on the French Riviera," the BBC reported. "He suffered the fatal seizure at approximately 1100 local time (1000GMT). The artist who had lived in seclusion for some years is reported to have suffered from influenza during the winter but continued to paint. He was making plans for more than 200 pieces of his work to be shown at an art museum in Avignon next month. Last year to mark his 90th birthday the Louvre Museum in Paris staged a Picasso retrospective - the first time the work of a living artist had been exhibited. Tributes for Picasso have been pouring in. The sculptor Henry Moore said that Picasso was probably one of the most naturally gifted artists since Raphael. France's culture minister, Maurice Druou, said Picasso filled his century with his colours."

When Picasso died, something much bigger than that stocky 5 feet 2 inch man disappeared forever. It was both the death of modern art and the birth of a new modern art, where everything that came after would be judged to the work Picasso left behind. In his death was born a myth, even if he had already created and supported his own folk lore while still living and breathing. When deceased however, the legend would only enhance, the work would be held up with more reverence and his name alone would define what it is to be an artist, a compulsive creator, a genius.

Depending on whom you believe, Picasso's final years were either sad and unfulfilled or fittingly apt. After all, he had found the loyal woman to whom he was king, the same woman who said she did not need to look at the sun when she had Pablo Picasso in her life. Even if it was she who kept the old friends and family away, she at least kept Picasso going in the process; vital, relevant, alive and working right to the end. Was it a final chapter lived with satisfaction? Perhaps not, but it was one lived with the kind of wide eyed wonderment he had had since his boyhood in Malaga, the life of an explorer of the soul, an adventurer of the human psyche, a passionate scientist and thinker whose work told us more about what it is to be human than any other artist ever could. Flawed, loveable, head strong, bullish and charismatic, Picasso was all this and more to the very end, the king of his domain and the medium he chose to express himself within, the one he dominated for seventy years.

In the end, one might hope Picasso tied up a lot of loose ends within himself. Ideally, the restless womaniser found peace with his loving wife, at least it might seem that way from the outside looking in. Undoubtedly though, he left many things unsaid, many people hurt and a few of them damaged beyond repair. Whether it was down to him directly or their mere involvement with him, a man too big for any room to contain him, tragedy came in the wake of his death, as he himself had predicted.

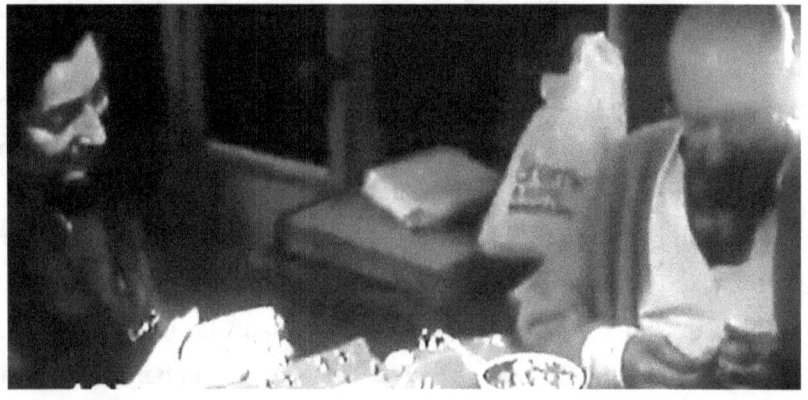

Opening presents on his last Christmas.

"Marie-Thérèse and Pablo had talked again on the telephone only a week before he died," Pablo's grandson Olivier Widmaier recalled recently, "four years earlier, in 1973. She had noticed that he was not well and had warned Maya, her feeling confirmed by the very feeble handwriting of Pablo's last letter, which had arrived on the morning of the telephone call. With his death their bond was finally broken."

Not everyone got to say their final goodbye however. Picasso's oldest friend, the 97 year old Manuel Pallares, heard the news on the radio in Barcelona and headed over as soon as he could. When he arrived at Picasso's home, Notre Dame de Vie, there were hounds snarling and guards at the gate. Despite their long and rich friendship, the old man was turned away, cruelly, coldly. Manuel was not the only one refused entry either; Maya, Claude and Paloma were also unable to get in and see their father, and his grandchildren

Pablito and Marina would not be allowed to attend the funeral. It was strictly a private affair.

The funeral began early, with the hearse holding his body and widow setting off out of Mougins at 5 in the morning, bound for Vauvenargues where he would be buried. His son Paulo was following the coffin in his car, along with Picasso's barber Aria, and his secretary Miguel; clearly, only the very trusted few. Marie-Therese called Miguel on the phone, and seeing as she was not allowed to see Pablo, asked him to give his body a kiss before they buried him. While Picasso was being buried, bizarre happenings took place. His grandson Pablito begged to be allowed to be present, but the drunken Paulo flat out refused, saying Jacqueline forbade it. Heartbroken, Pablito drank a bottle of bleach and was immediately rushed to hospital. His organs were eaten away, and within a couple of months he too, like his famous grandfather, was dead. Marie-Therese tried desperately to save him, even selling some of her Picasso artworks to pay the costs of various skin graft operations, but to no avail. It was a tragic end for the young man.

The settling of his estate from the word go was chaotic, and Picasso certainly left behind a huge mess, with children, former lovers, wives and associates battling it out for their rightful share of the fortune. As with any rich man's death, there was a lot at stake, but as Picasso had moved on so many times in his life, cut people out and loose, the whole affair was a shambles. To this day, there are rumblings of discontent about how the money was shared. More than money though, is the sheer weight of Picasso's legacy, and how it went on to affect those who had once been closer to him. He was like a ghost haunting them, refusing to disappear.

121

More tragedy was to come of course. Paulo, his first son, died at the age of 54 in 1975, only two years after his iconic father. Even more grim and bleak things followed. Though Picasso had a legacy of great art, he also had a legacy of despair and destruction. The man who painted Guernica calling for world peace caused serious unrest, either deliberately or through the fact that the women in his life became dependant on his aura to the point of obsession. Indeed, Pablo has bloody, grizzly scenarios forever attached to his name.

In October of 1977, Marie-Therese, the woman Picasso had once wanted for himself when she was on the brink of adulthood decades earlier, hanged herself in her garage at the age of 68. Explaining her mother's sad death, Maya later said that Picasso dying was almost too much for her. "She felt she had to look after him, even when he was dead," was Maya's sad conclusion.

The most heartbreaking event occurred in October of 1986, thirteen years after her husband died, when Jacqueline, hours before she was to appear at the Art Museum in Madrid for a Picasso exhibition, shot herself in the head with a pistol. It mirrored the event that triggered Picasso's Blue Period over eighty years earlier, the suicide of Casagemas. The tragedy had come full circle, but this suicide was perhaps the most tragic aspect of the Picasso tale, that the woman who claimed she could not live without her beloved husband proved it one fateful day, taking her own life to join Picasso in the everlasting.

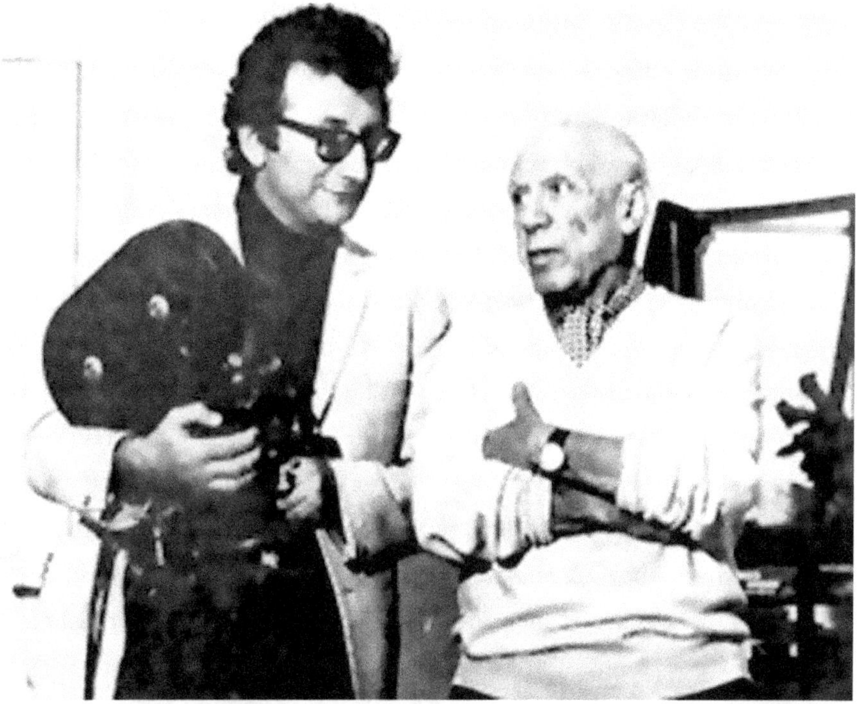

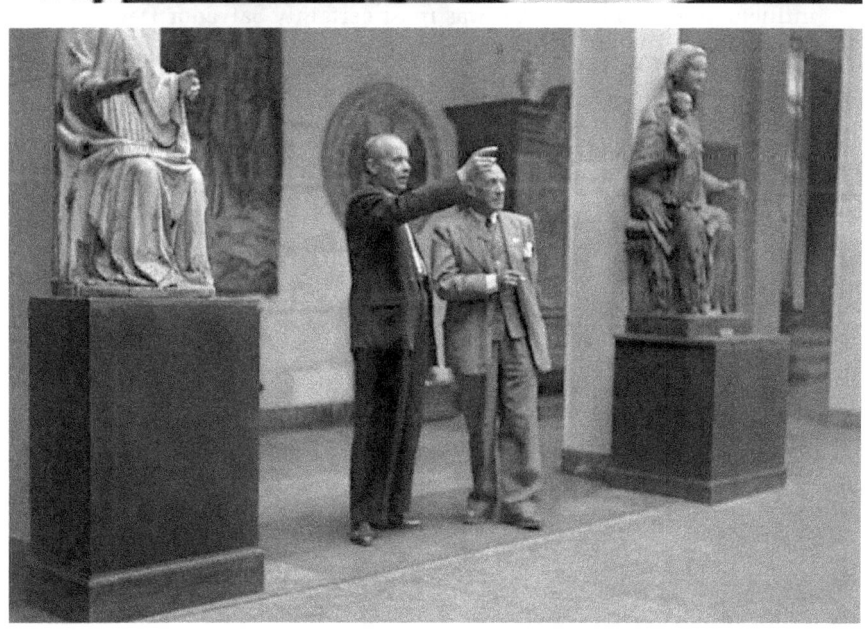

Picasso had been so alive, so full of passion and energy for all of his 91 years that it is hard to swallow that his body could just simply give in. It does, effectively, remind one of life's fragility, that even such a man, as hard as he might try, can not fight off death, though he did quite a good job for a while. By keeping the passion and joy in his life - as much he could anyway - he kept his heart pumping, the blood flowing, the eyes seeing and the soul feeling. Given that Picasso is so often elevated to God like status, it is easy to forget that he was a mere mortal. He was, after all, "just" an artist, but an important one all the same. Artists can often tell us more about ourselves than anyone else, and though they are not performing heart surgery or saving lives, they are making sense of them, even if they could not always make sense of their own. In the end, when Picasso died, there was no one to take his place. The largest personality and most influential artist in his wake was most certainly Salvador Dali, but by 1973 he was hardly as vital or prolific as Picasso had been, even in his final days. Clearly, no one could replace Picasso, and every artist, whether they liked to admit it or not, was now standing in his foreboding shadow.

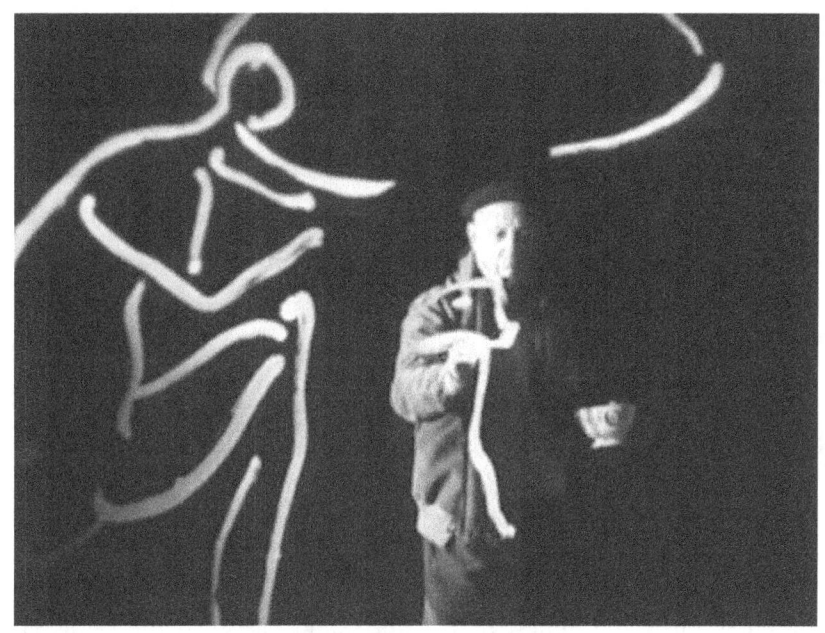

THE FINAL WORD

The Legacy of Picasso's Later Years

"Genius is a term that seems to be used very often today. But it's true
in his case, and you really need to plunge into his work fully to
understand that term."

- Picasso's granddaughter, Diana Widmaier Picasso

It's fitting that Picasso often said art was not made to decorate walls,
but to use as a weapon to shock and challenge. Even today, 45 years
after his death, his work continues to outrage, impress and inform
new generations who weren't even born when he was in his final
years, me among them. The life of Picasso is often told through his

art, and when told through his biographical timeline (i.e. his wives, homes, friends and children), the tale often becomes depressing, repeated, grim even. With his art though, it becomes colourful, vibrant and illustrious, but also dark, bleak and unflinching. His work is the unofficial historical document of almost all the twentieth century, told through many shades, many styles, many moods; war, peace, torment, love, sex, obsession, power, hunger, and finally, death.

Picasso's legacy is forever brought up as not only important in art, but in general history. To children being taught about art and introduced to its splendour, Picasso is always one of the first few names that come up. After all, he painted like a child, and that is why his work gets to our most basic feelings. It's in the simplicity, the purity, the honesty, his distinct lack of pretension, the bold colours, the daring bravery, the arrogance, the shamelessness. Children are often so open and honest that it hurts, and Picasso is the same. He channels our rawest qualities, and reflects them right back at us. His work was not only his own personal diary, but a diary for the world to read, a book of the soul forever worth drawing inspiration from.

As for those related to him, Picasso's legacy is monumental. "My grandfather only began to come to life for me the day he died," Olivier Widmaier Picasso told the Guardian. "8 April 1973. It was a Sunday afternoon, and after lunch we were watching a film on television. At the end, there was a special newsflash. I knew what that meant: some sort of disaster, a terrorist attack, the death of some famous person. There was no picture, but an unemotional voice intoned: 'The painter Pablo Picasso passed away this morning at his home on the Côte d'Azur. He was 92. He was generally held to be the artist who invented 20th-century art.' At school, I became an object of curiosity. Picasso's grandson! But life went on and Picasso became an institution."

Diana Widmaier Picasso, daughter of the great Maya, has also had to come to terms with her grandfather's fame and mountainous reputation, but she has become an art historian, looking after his legacy. "As a child I was always passionate about art. I did theater, played music, took dancing classes. I was aware that my grandfather was very famous and that he was a painter, but then it took me a while to understand his real genius. It was not really overshadowing. It was something that gave me freedom to learn about art. I would have loved to know him, of course, but I think it's important to get different opinions of people who knew him and then I can build my own reality. He's a man of many faces. So even if I knew him, I'm not quite sure which face he would have shown me."

As for Picasso's later years, only now are these works getting the credit they deserve, and though the period when he was in his seventies through to his nineties has often been overlooked, these years are in my view an essential part of his story. Without the end, there is really no beginning and no middle. The adventures, art and personal experiences Picasso had from the 1950s to the early 1970s make for fascinating reading; they remain contradictory, paradoxical and poignant, while the work he created in these eras was just as vibrant and intense as his earlier, more celebrated work. Now, the finale makes a little more sense, it being a poetic curtain call for a life lived to the full. Forty years on from his death, we are only just starting to catch up with him.

References and Acknowledgements

Thanks to Isabel Coulton for getting me in touch with her mother, Lydia Corbett, and of course to Lydia herself for talking to me about the Picasso Sylvette paintings.

Books;
Picasso: Creator and Destroyer, by Arianna Stassinopoulos
Pablo Picasso, Taschen
Portrait of Picasso, by Roland Penrose
Life with Picasso, by Francoise Gilot
The Success and Failure of Picasso, by John Berger
Picasso: Late Years, RH Wilenski
Picasso; His Late Works
Picasso, by Roland Penrose
Forever Picasso, by Roberto Otero
Picasso; The Last Years, by Gert Schiff

Documentaries and footage;
BBC Modern Masters, Picasso
Picasso's Last Stand
Picasso: Love, Sex and Art
Picasso: Magic, Sex and Death
Matisse Meets Picasso
Picasso: The Legacy of a Genius
Picasso: War, Peace and Love
Maya Picasso Interview, for Mystery of Picasso

Articles;

Lydia Corbett features, BBC and Fosse Gallery

The Guardian and Telegraph interviews with Francoise Gilot

Art News, Late Picasso

New York Times, Picasso: The Last Decade

London Review of Books, Tate Review 1988

Cahiers d'Art, 1935

Francois Truffaut on Mystery of Picasso

ABOUT CHRIS WADE

Chris Wade is a UK based writer, filmmaker, artist and musician. As well as running the acclaimed music project Dodson and Fogg, he has written books on The Kinks, Salvador Dali, Madonna, Captain Beefheart, Robert De Niro and many others. He has also released audiobooks of his comedic fiction, such as Cutey and the Sofaguard, narrated by Rik Mayall. His other projects include Rainsmoke, a musical outfit with actor Nigel Planer, and Hound Dawg Magazine, for which he has interviewed such people as Sharon Stone, Donovan and Jethro Tull's Ian Anderson. His art films, The Apple Picker (accepted by Sydney World Film Festival, featuring Toyah Willcox and Nigel Planer), and Seven Days in Never, were filmed and released in 2017.

More info at his website: wisdomtwinsbooks.weebly.com

www.ingramcontent.com/pod-product-compliance
Lightning Source LLC
Chambersburg PA
CBHW071447180526
45170CB00001B/494